LOVE SONGS OF

HEALING AND HOPE

July 2022

Dear Lynne,

Wishing you

every blessing,

Tim

British Library Cataloguing in Publication Data:
a catalogue record for this publication
is available from the British Library

© Fiona Gardner 2022

The right of Mrs Fiona Gardner to be identified as the author of this
work has been asserted by her in accordance with the Copyright,
Designs and Patents Act 1988

ISBN: 978-1-912052-73-8

Typeset in 11.5pt Minion Pro at Haddington, Scotland

Printed by West Port Print & Design, St Andrews

CONTENTS

All proceeds from this book will be split between two inspirational Charities: Quiet Waters, and Richmond's Hope. (This does not mean that either of these Charities supports the contents of this book.)

Quiet Waters provides listening and support services for all. They have a Christian ethos, and provide services to all irrespective of faith, gender, sexuality, ethnic origins or life choices. It is based in Falkirk and can be reached on 01324 630643 or https://quiet-waters.org

Richmond's Hope provides support for children and young people aged 4-18 years who have been bereaved. The charity provides a safe space for children to work through their grief both verbally and non-verbally, to help them preserve memories of the person who died, explore their feelings, develop coping strategies and to understand the impact the bereavement has had on their lives. It has offices in Glasgow and Edinburgh, and the website is https://www.richmondshope.org.uk

ACKNOWLEDGEMENTS

I am so grateful to all who have journeyed with me, and who have listened and prayed and supported – thank you. I especially want to thank Muriel, for her persistent prayers and encouragement, Sally for her understanding of what I am trying to do, Gail and Alan for their support and thoughtfulness and Margaret Whyte for her wisdom and insights.

I am grateful for all who have written – to Margaret, Linda, Lynsey, Fergus, Muriel, David, Lesli, Laura, Muriel and my son Andrew. You are such a blessing, such a creative crowd of people, with such inspirational stories and a desire to encourage others. A loving community.

I am so thankful too, for the support of many, including family and friends, especially Myra and Helen, Marianne, Johanna and David, Clare and Louise and Nancy, Alison, Bill and Brian, to Andy for helping with technical stuff, and to Jock, my editor and publisher for his patience and wisdom.

I write to try and make sense out of my journey through trauma, confusion and grief. There is so much I do not understand. In the midst of pandemic and conflicts in our world, it is so important that we know that there are others who will lovingly listen, and tenderly care and quietly support and pray. We are never alone, but have a God who sees us, and who wishes to encircle us with love, even when we feel broken, ashamed and hopeless. And so we continue to journey, and eventually find new strength, inspiration and even hope along the way.

Acknowledgements of permissions to quote are at the back.

> Therefore encourage one another and build each other up, just as in fact you are doing."
>
> *1 Thessalonians 3:11*

Section 1: AFTER THE WOUND

A bird does not sing because it has an answer, it sings because it has a song.

Chinese proverb

God heals the broken hearted and binds up their wounds.

Psalm 147:3

After my husband died, on the 14th April 2018, I was distraught – not just because he had passed away, but because of how much he had suffered when he was alive. Colin experienced a head injury when he served in the military, and developed degenerative epilepsy as a result. His journey of trauma, epilepsy and cognitive decline was dramatic and often destructive. His Christian faith and desire to do the right thing sustained him, but it was all raw, unpredictable and horribly messy.

Colin always wanted to tell his story, through his poems and writings, and because he was not well enough, he never finished. So it seemed the best thing I could do to honour his memory, was to pick up the fragments of his writings, and place them in context, so that they could be understand and appreciated. And I was so glad to be able to do so. In some ways it was bleak work, because it stirred up so many painful memories. Yet it also reminded me of the joy on the journey – times of grace, humour, kindness and insight. In my first years after Colin's death, putting these stories together gave me a purpose, a way of seeking something good to come out of the heartache. I wanted to tell his story, to raise awareness of the plight of veterans, and to raise money for two charities – 'Epilepsy Connections' and 'The Coming Home Centre' in Govan.

I am a very private person by nature, so writing *Love Song for a Wounded Warrior* was tough, but then holding the book launch in June 2020 by zoom was excruciating. It was like doing your washing in public. I found that I had to pray for God to give me courage, as I was so very fearful and worried that we would be judged. I was so relieved at having so many understanding people around – people who were supportive and full of grace. It was so healing just to be heard.

What I hadn't counted on however, was what would happen next. I was able to tell Colin's story at Remembrance 2020 in various ways, which was a great privilege. However I discovered that in some ways, focussing on telling Colin's story had actually served as a distraction from my own healing. The death of Colin's parents – his dad in October 2019 and then his mum in January 2020, added layers of grief, and every time I tried to make progress, I seemed to go backwards. My world has changed so much it is almost unrecognisable, and I feel a deep sense of loss and yearning for the past, of a rhythm of life that is now unavailable, and a sense of being incomplete.

Another aspect of my journey, which was unexpected, was that I started to blog – *anumbrellaofhealinglove*. I wrote about aspects of my struggles, which I thought might be helpful to others. The idea was that somehow by telling my own story, maybe this would be an encouragement to others, that under the umbrella we would find shelter and mutual healing. In the course of doing this, I discovered some new and unexpected things. First that I loved writing, I really enjoy it. It has become a blessing in itself. However what I discovered through writing, was that the wound was much deeper than I knew. It has surprised me is how long it has taken to feel a bit better, and I wanted to give other people permission to know that it takes as long as it takes, and can't be hurried. That is deeply frustrating.

I think my grief from the death of Colin and his parents, my vicarious trauma at listening to and living with Colin, and being his carer, had affected my life much more deeply than I had realised. The residue of trauma can bring many issues, including poor boundaries and self esteem and fearful and damaged patterns of thinking. During his life, so many of my decisions were made based on trying to care for Colin, and to give him the best quality of life, I had forgotten how to make decisions for myself or my own wellbeing. The healing process of trying to work this through has been incredibly challenging, and I get it wrong all the time. The realisation of the impact of long term trauma and complex grief has been a revelation, and not of a good kind! It is a daily battle.

If the wound has been much deeper than I knew, another surprising consequence of all this is that God has given me a new community around me. I have been privileged to get to know new people who have walked with me on my journey, who have shared their stories and who have been a great blessing. People have got in touch with me to share something of their stories and I have so welcomed this. As we have shared together, it feels as if there has been a safety net of care and community formed, and that has been a real encouragement. Especially in this time of pandemic when people have been isolated from each other, it has been good to be able to connect, through prayer, social media, phone calls and at times even visits in the rain in the garden! It has deepened my understanding of how much people need to be heard in safe places. There is so much pain and trauma that can occur, lives saturated with anger and shame and ugliness, which need to be brought into the light, so people can find acceptance and healing. There are many in today's society, who because of stress, trauma or family problems really need a word of encouragement and appreciation.

The pandemic has exacerbated this by making people more isolated, and this includes key workers, the bereaved and veterans and their families. People have functioned under enormous stress, and so these writings are offered as a resource that might help in days of exhaustion and desolation.

After I had written *Love Song for a Wounded Warrior*, some of the feedback that I had was that it was a hard book to read. In places it was just a relentless round of trauma, hospital appointments and disability. I wrote it like this, because that is what it was. In the midst of it, though, was also laughter, ridiculous antics, moments of connection, and much inspiration and kindness. I tried to include this too!

I feel that in some ways the story was only half told, so I wanted to balance things out by writing *Love Songs for Healing and Hope*, for people who feel wounded and scarred by life's battles. I want to publish this as a series of honest reflections, and to say that we are not alone, and that there is hope. I am very aware that everyone's experiences of grief and life are very individual, and that these reflections are not for everyone. I write as a Christian, but this book is for anyone, people of faith and of none, for I believe that God cherishes every human being, and wants every person to be touched by love, and to be whole.

Ultimately for me, my love song is inspired by God, by hearing snatches of a heavenly love song, which has consoled me, and strengthened and inspired me along the way. I still have so much to learn, and have a number of holes in my soul. Yet I believe that God is healing me and giving me hope, and helping me find my true identity, after years of confusion and soulful searching.

And so I write to encourage others. I believe that no one is ever too broken to be beyond God's mercy and possibilities of healing, no matter what has happened. May we continue to listen, to encourage, to pray and to learn, so we can form a community of healing and grace for all who struggle.

To say a little more about *Love Songs for Healing and Hope*: there are three aspects to this book – first, section two has some of the **blogs** I have published about the struggles and difficulties of living with trauma and grief. Next, in section three I have invited some beautiful friends to share something of their own **stories**, and of the things that made a difference for them. I have learned so much from others in this community of grace, I thought it would be good for more of these stories and insights to be heard. Third, section four has some practical **resources** offered to support those who are grieving or feel overwhelmed, including bible verses and contemporary songs. Then there are some meditations on various biblical figures on the theme of love, included in a final section. The whole book is offered as resource to bring healing and grace to others, even on the darkest of nights.

An image that keeps occurring to me, is from Zephaniah:

> The Lord your God is with you,
> he is mighty to save.
> he will take great delight over you,
> he will quiet you with his love,
> he will rejoice over you with singing.
>
> *Zephaniah 3:17*

There are times in life, when we feel that we don't have the strength to keep going. There are times when we feel that we have messed up one time too many. There are times when the fear and burdens of this world seem too heavy. Our hearts break, and our tears just keep falling.

It is when we are at our very lowest, that God reminds us that we do not suffer alone, for he is with us. He takes us to the green pastures, where we find nourishment, to the quiet streams, where we find rest. He reminds us that we are always seen, always heard. And even just in that place of brokenness, God sees us and takes delight in our existence, and quietens our hurting souls with his love. Like a mother quietening a wailing child, so God comes to us, to soothe and quieten our souls.

And then he chooses to sing over us. When we are disorientated and overcome with sorrow, dysregulated as they say, God comes to us and sings a lullaby. And we don't need to respond by filling in a questionnaire or doing six good things before breakfast. Instead all we need to do is to stop and listen. And the singing of God, his love song to us, is beautiful. The melody blesses us and the notes inspire hope. The sound heals us of our jagged edges and sores, and inspires us with the astounding power and goodness of God, and the new possibilities that there can be for the future, a new song.

I am not a therapist or a counsellor, so I offer these resources as a fellow human being, seeking to find meaning, and some kind of healing and peace. In these days following the pandemic, there is still much disconnection and fear, it feels as if this makes this process so much harder. Many are going through times of strain, brokenness and grief. I want to offer a book of resources, which if it resonates with just one person, and makes you laugh, or gives you permission to cry, then it will have achieved its purpose. Grief can be so complex, and affects life so profoundly – sometimes we laugh hysterically to relieve tension, at other times we wrestle with guilt and regrets. **However you are feeling, you are not alone, you are loved and there is hope.**

When old words die out on the tongue,
new melodies break forth from the heart,
and where the old tracks are lost,
new country is revealed with its wonders.

Rabindranath Tagore

Themes in the Midst of the Process

> Praise be to the God and Father of our Lord Jesus Christ, the Father of compassion, and the God of all comfort, who comforts us in all our troubles, so we can comfort those in any trouble with the comfort we ourselves have received from God.
>
> *2 Corinthians 1:3-4*

> Tell me and I forget, teach me and I may remember, involve me, and I learn.
>
> *probably Confucius first*

Julia Margaret Cameron suggests that growth is a spiral process, doubling back on itself. After Colin's death, I thought naively, that after a period of being sad, I would then gradually heal and feel better. Needless to say, this has not been my experience! Colin had been ill for such a very long time, with struggles over military memories, epilepsy and resulting brain injury: I thought surely I had already done much of my grieving. I had watched Colin struggle for many years, at home and in a care home. I had tried to support him and love him, and I thought after he died that I would begin to find my way.

While Helen Keller used to say that the world is not only full of suffering, but full of its overcoming, my journey towards healing and hope has been much tougher than I could have imagined. I have at times gone round in circles, sometimes been overwhelmed by pain, and wondered who I am. I have struggled not just with my husband's death, but also in processing some of the memories around his struggle for life and behavioural issues. Then both Colin's parents, his dad and then his mum passed away, in 2019 and then 2020. They were both incredibly supportive of us as a family, and although they were both well into their 90s, their loss compounded my grief. This perhaps sounds selfish – they had lived long, creative and full lives, but I miss them. In seeking to support Colin, we had all loved fiercely and at times recklessly, but we had done this together. There are few people left to talk through these memories.

I think in the first year after Colin's death, I was a bit numb. I had to attend to practical and legal matters, which took a lot of my energy. I think I often tried to approach things in a pragmatic way, and tried to do things without really realising that this was too much too soon. God had a way of slowing me down, when just about a week after Colin's funeral, I managed to break a bone in my foot, in the cinema of all places! I had to be still, which was not easy, but I needed to have time out and to rest. I had not realised how exhausted I was.

I was so grateful for people who helped me in these days, Sally and Jim, Gail and Alan, and the Bield at Blackruthven, who provided me with shelter when I needed a sage and loving place to be. The broken bone in my foot somehow symbolised my broken heart, and somehow the two needed a time of rest and space before I could begin to process. I think often after a bereavement, we are exhausted from caring and doing practical things, and our bodies need time to rest, and our souls need space to process and catch up.

In the second year, I started to try to collate all of Colin's writings, and to put them into some kind of order and to try to explain how his injuries from his military service affected his whole life. This was a constructive way to honour his memory, but also in some ways was a distraction from my own grief. My third year was focusing on my own path to healing, and to ask God to help me heal from difficult memories and negative patterns of thought, and to rediscover my identity. I am grateful to have had good support in this process. I am aware that at times there are setbacks, with times of stress or exhaustion, which can be discouraging. I guess in any process there can be backward steps, but after time to regroup, you seek to persevere again on the path.

In my pain and questioning, different themes kept emerging, and I want to share some of them with you.

1 The consequences of being a carer

Love is unselfishly choosing for another's higher good.

(source unknown)

Love is patient, love is kind. It does not envy, it does not boast, it is not proud. It does not dishonour others, it is not self-seeking, it is not easily angered, it keeps no record of wrongs. Love does not delight in evil but rejoices with the truth. It always protects, always trusts, always hopes, always perseveres.

1 Corinthians 13:4-8

To care for another human being is such a great privilege – it helps you understand the nature of love, to try and look after someone when they are unwell and maybe cranky and difficult! It can be hugely rewarding and also deeply challenging. After many years of caring for Colin within the house, Colin's condition continued to deteriorate, he was having seizures and seizure activity, and his behaviours became more erratic.

For Colin, after a further degeneration in his health, and a hospital stay, it became apparent that he needed full time care, and he was admitted into a care home with a unit for young adults with physical disabilities. I am so grateful that such places exist, as Colin was too young to be in a care home for senior citizens, and he benefited immensely to have specialised care for his complex needs. Eileen Docherty and her team in Adam's unit in Craigielea care home loved and looked after Colin exceptionally well.

I am writing about this theme, because being a carer over a long period of time is exhausting, and you can become a different person without even noticing, for the change happens so gradually. When the person is in the house, you are on high alert, watching for behavioural changes or fluctuations in health. You are constantly adapting to different scenarios. You co-ordinate carers and prescriptions and hospital appointments. You work and look after family – and the danger is that you lose yourself in exhaustion and stress. The mundane nature of chores and caring can take over.

Visiting and supporting a loved one in a hospital setting can be a bit confusing, just because although there are lots of great medical staff, sometimes they use a language which is difficult to relate to. At times it can feel that you are hearing contradictory information. I think it is always good to ask questions, and where needed to be an advocate on behalf of the patient. Asking for a second opinion, to speak to the nurse in charge of a ward, or a consultant, if you feel something is wrong or you are worried, can be so helpful. It can make something a bit clearer, or provide a crucial piece of information which could inform treatment and care.

When you are worried about a loved one, it can be hard to take in all that a medical person is saying, sometimes you need time to think about things, to realise some piece of the jigsaw might be more relevant than you thought, or to take a decision about treatment options. If you are able, to take someone with you to be a co-listener, can also be helpful, or to take notes. It can be hard to find that balance between following your instincts, and integrating that with the medical information available, to work out the best course of action in any given circumstances.

When Colin went into Craigielea Care Home, I was so thankful that he was so well looked after, but there was also a lot of guilt and tears. It was excruciating to do, but was the best choice of the ones that were possible. I sympathise so much with people who have to make these kind of decisions. Family and friends visited Colin often – and I am so grateful for all involved in this. Even the dog could visit!

It was only in the years after Colin's death, without the responsibility of caring for Colin, and seeing his mum and dad, I realised that I had forgotten how to *be*, or remember what I liked or disliked, or how to make choices. When you are immersed in someone else's care, you almost forget you are a person, and this is how you cope. I have many things that I would like to have done better, I got lots of things wrong in trying to care for Colin. But because so much of my identity for so long was as a carer, somewhere along the way I lost much of my sense of self.

I mention this, because I wonder if this is true for others? It is not that you would do things any differently, in terms of love or commitment – just that afterwards your grief is not just for the person who has died, but also for the person you used to be. And I think that person doesn't come back. They do say that you become a more grounded person through it all, with a greater sympathy for others! That is indeed a heartening thought.

When seeking to discover more of my identity, I have been reading some of the work of Brene Brown – such as her books *Gifts from Imperfection* and *Braving the Wilderness*. Brene quotes words from Maya Angelou:

> You only are free when you realize you belong no place — you belong every place — no place at all. The price is high, the reward is great.[1]

We need to know who we are, when we are not with others, influenced by them or by our context. And I think part of my journey just now, is to rediscover my sense of identity and my freedom. I know that I am a daughter of God, and I am loved. But I think I also need times of silence and stillness, when I can learn to 'belong to myself' as Brene speaks of, and find inner cohesion and a greater sense of wholeness.

> True belonging is the spiritual practice of believing in and belonging to yourself so deeply that you can share your most authentic self with the world and find sacredness both in being part of something and standing alone in the wilderness. True belonging doesn't require you to change who you are: it requires you to be who you are.[2]

There is something so profound here, for often we are most true to ourselves when we are by ourselves, and the challenge is to be ourselves when in a crowd. It takes a lot of work sometimes, because I think our image of ourselves can get distorted by our experiences in life, especially childhood experiences. Negative words and attitudes often remain in our memories, and shape our understanding of ourselves, and especially our self worth. It is good to be able to work through these, to find healing and freedom. Books like *Healing your Lost Inner Child* by Robert Jackman can give insights into this kind of journey.

It is not an easy task, to learn to be at peace with yourself. Marianne Williamson says,

> It takes courage ... to endure the sharp pains of self-discovery rather than choose to take the dull pain of unconsciousness that would last the rest of our lives.[3]

---

1 Brene Brown, *Braving the Wilderness*, Penguin Random House, 5.
2 Brown, *Braving the Wilderness*, 40.
3 Marianne Williamson, *A Return to Love*, Harper Collins (Goodreads).

There is something important about retaining your identity where possible, and then consciously seeking to rediscover it when it becomes tarnished or lost, so that after years of caring, we can find a deeper sense of identity and peace.

2 Forgiveness of self and of other

> Be kind and compassionate to one another, forgiving each other, just as in Christ, God forgave you.
>
> *Ephesians 4:31-32*

When trying to support someone with complex needs and behavioural issues, it is really tough. I think you are torn apart, because part of you is with the person, knows their story, and how they react to things. You see the world through their eyes, their helplessness, frustration with their disability, their scepticism about officialdom. You are their advocate in a world of health and social care, trying to be there for them, and to get the best care needed. Yet at times there is not an obvious fit, and everyone feels let down. One of the most pressing examples of that was when Colin went into hospital. He often had an infection, having seizures, and was not able to speak for himself, and trying to communicate his needs in a way that was heard, was so very difficult. Colin's needs were so complex, and in a busy acute medical ward, the nuances of my perceptions of his progress were not always well received.

I tried to be prayerful and patient, and I met many caring people along the way, who took into account Colin's situation and were attentive to him. Sometimes his brain damage meant he was also very difficult, angry and disruptive, and this was harder still. I was always apologising, but asking that medical staff would realise that this was part of his condition. People who were reassuring to him, patient, who listened and tried to explain what was happening, were such a blessing. Their efforts were not always well received by Colin, but if there was anything likely to have a good outcome this was it. People who overlooked social niceties, who diffused tension with humour, who saw beyond the angry person before them, and the deeper needs of fear, confusion and trauma, who treated Colin as a valued person with a story, were so helpful. With these people there was a dignity and connectivity that at times could overcome tensions and a difficult mood.

For the most part, I think we were all understanding of each other. Colin and I knew in our souls that we were all trying to do the best thing for each other, but at times we were at odds. He was trying to forgive himself for some of the things he did in the military. I was trying to forgive myself for not being able to look after him in the house. I thought about stopping working, and trying to be more present, but that would have solved very little, as he slept a lot, kept unusual hours and was unpredictable. At times he couldn't understand why I didn't side with him more regarding what he thought he needed, and as time went on his perception of life became distorted and damaged. There were times that I needed to take decisions for his own protection and wellbeing, that he didn't understand or appreciate, and this was tough. There were times when he was hostile towards me, because although I was sympathetic to his world view, I couldn't always comply with his conclusions or act upon them.

When we look at our lives, it is hard not to beat ourselves up. If I had approached things another way, would that have made a difference? If I had only tried to get different support, would that have helped Colin? I struggle with guilt that I missed something. Sometimes Colin just wanted to be miserable by himself. Should I have tried harder? When I chose to have time off or see a friend, it might have helped me retain a vestige of humanity, but what if I was out when he had a seizure? There are no good answers, but lots of compromises where every choice is tainted by being not enough. Trying to forgive oneself is difficult.

Verses about forgiveness help: 'As far as the east is from the west, so far has he removed our transgressions from us' (Psalm 103:12) or 'The Lord is forgiving and merciful (Daniel 9:9) can help to release us from guilt. We also have to discern if the sense of guilt is proportionate and true, or a false guilt – just the way we punish ourselves. We need to be released from false guilt, but to take ownership of what is ours. If Jesus could forgive others, whilst hanging on a cross, then I need to forgive even myself, and also to trust that God is still good, even when I don't understand.

At times I was angry, especially when Colin had a number of seizures together in the middle of the night, and I knew it would take him weeks to recover, and that there would be more brain damage as a result. It seemed so cruel, that the sheer volume and relentless severity of seizures caused such devastation to a human soul. I would pray that he wouldn't have another seizure, and then often he did. I just wanted relief for him, and for all of us, but it was not to be.

I usually managed to cover my frustrations with a veneer of civility. Something inside me became numb to allow me to keep going. At times it was easier not to hope, because then I wasn't disappointed. I didn't have much time to be emotionally engaged with others around, as just surviving, working, looking after my son was more than enough. We did have some lovely family times, especially in the early years, when Andrew was young, and that was great. I took lots of photos in graced moments, just to help me remember.

I have worked hard to forgive those who let Colin down, and deal with the times when I let him down. Having regrets about the past, or becoming bitter only makes the wound sting more. I need to let go, so that the wound can heal and the scar form. The scar is not pretty, but at least the wound is no longer open.

There is a beautiful song by Casting Crowns called 'Scars in heaven' which reminds us that in heaven our wounds are so completely healed, that the only scars are those of Jesus. And there is a beautiful lyric which says where the singer talks of a loved one:

> There is a wound here in my heart where something's missing,
> and they tell me it's going to heal with time
> but I know you're in a place where all your wounds are erased,
> and knowing yours are healed, is healing mine.

We pray for all carers, whose loved one is departed, that they find this kind of self-forgiveness and healing, so that they in turn can find peace.

3 The impact of trauma

In the early days after Colin's death, when I was talking about how I felt about life, a friend suggested that I read a book by Bessel van der Kolk, *The Body Keeps the Score*, and reading this book was life changing for me in my understanding of the impact that trauma can have on people, and of different ways we can try to process it. We all experience trauma in life, i.e. distressing events that happen which have long term effects. I discovered that trying to support Colin, as well as listening to his many retellings of traumatic events, had left me with vicarious trauma, in that I had listened to these events so often, that I felt I had lived through them.

Part of my journey was to go to the annual Trauma Conference in Boston in June 2019, where I learned more about the nature of trauma and how people can learn to find greater peace. I have learned so much from some of the speakers, people like Bessel van der Kolk and Bruce Perry, and the importance of feeling safe, loved and supported, in terms of relationships and human interactions. I have needed to work very intentionally on my recovery, acknowledging and working through these traumatic memories. I still have so much to learn.

The quotations about trauma that I have most resonated with, are the following:

> Traumatized people chronically feel unsafe inside their bodies: the past is alive in the form of gnawing interior discomfort. Their bodies are constantly bombarded by visceral warning signs, and, in an attempt to control these processes, they often become expert at ignoring their gut feelings and in numbing awareness of what is played out inside. They learn to hide from their selves.[4]

My idea of trauma used to be that for example it was a startle reflex to a loud noise. However I learned that actually it impacts every part of you – it's about not feeling safe, and struggling to interpret the proportionality of what is going on internally, as well as how you relate to the world. Another quotation explains this so well:

> We have learned that trauma is not just an event that took place sometime in the past; it is also the imprint left by that experience on mind, brain, and body. This imprint has ongoing consequences for how the human organism manages to survive in the present. Trauma results in a fundamental reorganization of the way mind and brain manage perceptions. It changes not only how we think and what we think about, but also our very capacity to think.[5]

---

4   Bessel van der Kolk, *The Body Keeps the Score*, Penguin, 96-7.
5   Van der Kolk, *The Body Keeps the Score*, 21.

This understanding has made me revisit how we relate to one another as human beings. I am just learning about trauma-informed practice, but I want to know more, as it seems the wisest way to relate to others, whatever their background. People can open up and learn to trust, only when we respect their need for choice, safety and empowerment.

Often people think that if they can just speak in an authoritarian style or loud voice, that this will help when someone is distressed. However while it might work in some situations, I believe it can also be counterproductive, for it can make things worse. Bessel says:

> One thing is certain: yelling at someone who is already out of control can only lead to further dysregulation. Just as your dog cowers if you shout and wags his tail when you speak in a high singsong, we humans respond to harsh voices with fear, anger, or shutdown and to playful tones by opening up and relaxing. We simply cannot help but respond to these indicators of safety or danger.[6]

When I think of how Colin responded to the difficult experiences of conflict and war, and subsequently to loud noises or crowds, these above quotations were so true. The memories that Colin kept reliving were so devastating, that they changed his identity and how he related to the world, so that he felt of little value; he could have very black moods, and could be on edge. He didn't feel safe.

For those of us around Colin, we had an intuitive understanding of this, but it was so hard to work out how he was responding to any situation, and what response from us would help him feel less agitated and calmer. I heard Colin's stories so often – car bombs, shootings etc, that I felt as if I had been there too, so then I have had to learn to find constructive ways of processing this vicarious trauma.

Some of the most effective ways can be neurolinguistic programming or EMDR (Eye Movement Desensitisation and Reprocessing). There are many things that can be helpful – especially exercise and body work such as trauma-informed yoga, capacitar and community activities where you can find your voice through singing or drama. Different combinations can work for different people, but the important thing is that there are

---

6   Van der Kolk, *The Body Keeps the Score*, 85.

possibilities to heal. For Colin, I wish I had understood more about these trauma therapy options earlier on, to see if they would have helped. It might be too late for him now, but not too late for others.

As an individual, I have tried to develop a self-awareness as to how I react to things, and recognise when it may be a trauma response. There are things I just don't want to do anymore, as I still get easily triggered by simple things into old memories. I don't want to watch war movies, there are associations I need to watch out for, that are still painful. There are practical things too. When Colin lived in the house, I couldn't have a window cleaner around, as Colin on a bad day would have seen that as an invasion of his space, and could have been hyper-reactive. Even now, I find it hard to have a regular window cleaner, as it seems too high risk. It is hard to leave behind old habits, no matter how illogical it is.

Prayer, reflection, talking, counselling and so many other therapeutic and holistic interventions can all help with the process of healing, in order to enable us to live in greater freedom.

Section 2: THE BLOGS (June 2020 – Feb 2022)

Writing can help us express a little of what is going on

Index

Blog 1: Sorrowful but Always Rejoicing (2 Corinthians 6:10)

6th June 2020

Friends, I have waited a long time before starting to blog. Often I have wondered what to say, and what my message is.

It is such a cliche that everyone has a story to tell, but it feels so essential to life and identity, that I want to try. I am a Christian who doesn't have all the answers. I love Jesus, and God the Father is my shelter, and his Holy Spirit is gently nudging me to be more creative, to get in touch with my true self, and to have the courage to articulate a little of what that means.

In my core self, I am a bridge builder, a reconciler, an encourager. I am deeply flawed, I make loads of mistakes, I get things wrong, and I feel down at times because I think myself inadequate to fulfil what I feel called to do. I wrestle with how to take things forward.

I am also frustrated with cliches in the Christian world – particularly about suffering and pain, e.g. 'God has sent you this to make you stronger'. When you are sad and tearing your hair out, and everything is falling apart, with a restless noisy toddler, or a sick husband, these words don't seem to help.

In Psalm 45 verse 1, the psalmist says:

> My heart is stirred by a noble theme,
> As I recite my verses for the King
> My tongue is the pen of a ready writer.

God has blessed me so much, even in dark and difficult days in my life, when things made no sense. He encouraged me, and gave me strength, and still brings me healing every day. In Glasgow, it is often raining, and God is like my umbrella, protecting me, keeping me safe, and enabling me to flower underneath his care. And so my blog is called 'an umbrella of healing love'. My prayer is that this blog might give space to others to reflect on where they care, to know God's abundant and compassionate love for themselves, and to connect with Jesus' healing love in a deeper way.

Wishing you Christ's healing love,

Fiona

An invitation to pray:

Gracious God, Father, Son and Holy Spirit,

I have so many questions, my heart is restless, I cry to you.

Lord Jesus Christ, reveal to me your heart of Love,

Shelter and heal me,

Holy Spirit help me find the wholeness I seek, Amen.

Blog 2: Love Song for a Wounded Warrior

13th June 2020

Dear friends, thanks so much for reading this. Like so many people, I have a desire to write, to connect. I want to tell people about the difference that Jesus' love makes, and to encourage others on the journey through life.

You may wonder what the strap line 'Love Song for a Wounded Warrior' means, and so I would like to explain a bit more, although it takes all the courage I can muster.

My husband Colin died just over two years ago, in April 2018 after a long time of ill health, as he had intractable epilepsy. Many people have epilepsy which is well controlled – but not him.

Colin had an head injury, sustained on active service, and this was the cause of his seizures. He had quite a journey in military and civilian life, seeking to live with his injury and its consequences. Colin wrote reflectively about how he felt, fragments that give insight as to some of the experiences that he had, and he always wanted these published.

To give his writings a framework, I tried to provide a context for these writings, about how Colin's disability affected his family, as we sought to love and support him. Including a piece from our son Andrew, these were the material for our book *Love Song for a Wounded Warrior* which we wrote about Colin's life – a story of sorrow, humour, frustration, anger, joy and thanksgiving!

We offer this story to the world, even though I am full of trepidation – it feels like a very personal story to share. Yet I am also relieved to finally be able to fulfil Colin's wishes and tell his story, and I pray that through this story, others might be encouraged – especially family and carers of veterans and people with disabilities, who can find that their road often looks bleak and rocky.

The things that helped us on our journey were God, prayer and encouragement, family and friends, music, forgiveness, understanding, medicine, oases of care of the way, and the knowledge that God never forgot us. These things were often all intertwined. PTSD symptoms added to the melee, and added an additional layer of confusion to deal with.

The booklaunch will be on the 24th of June on zoom, and I am prayeful that these writings might do some good, to encourage another family to persevere, to remind people that every story is significant, to raise awareness of issues for veterans, people with epilespy and their families, and to raise funds for charity. All proceeds from this book go to 'Epilepsy Connections', and the 'Coming Home Centre' in Govan. More to come on this . . .

A prayer:

> Dear God, the bible is a book of stories of ordinary people who placed their trust in you, who made mistakes, who struggled, who fell down, and then stood back up.
>
> Help us to reflect on our own story, to notice all you have done, and to be thankful.
>
> Help us listen attentively and tenderly to each other's stories, with prayer and deep care,
>
> as you have called us, Amen.

See the colour section for some photos of Colin and our family life

Blog 3: Apologies and Explanations!

20th June 2020

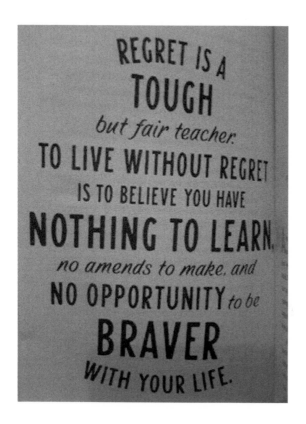

Brene Brown said, 'Regret is a tough but fair teacher'.[7]

Dear friends, when Colin said that he wanted his writings published, I can honestly say that I had no idea where this would lead. Colin wrote some poems and reflections on different incidents that happened to him in the military, but they were in fragmentary form. I felt that writing a framework for them would make more sense, and this framework became the story of Colin's life as a veteran in civilian life, and of the devastating

---

7   *Rising Strong*, Penguin Random House, 210.

impact that his history and disability had on him. This enables his story to be told in a fuller way.

Yet it is scary to tell this kind of story, because it is so very personal. And I am a very private person – as some of you know! So having the courage to do this, is immense. What I have discovered, is that it is easier for me to write this down, than to try and have a conversation about it all, as it is so complex, emotional, and at times harrowing.

And so I need to apologise to friends and colleagues who maybe feel bewildered that I didn't share more of Colin's story with them before. When I look back, it was easier to compartmentalise my life, in order to give it any semblance of normality. It was a relief at times to be out of the house, talking about normal things, to laugh, to play, and this space to be was literally a Godsend.

I have listened to other carers grappling with this issue, about not wanting to talk about a loved one's illness, especially when it is ongoing. It is easier to respond to the question, 'How is so and so?' with the response 'Up and down' than to give a long description of the details – e.g. for Colin – that he was affected by a seizure, depressed over memories from a military incident, or struggling with difficult behaviours because of a mood swing. There can be a lot of shame over difficult behaviours, and on many occasions I didn't have the energy to explain things to myself, never mind anyone else.

In these years, I was blessed with a small but lovely group of supportive and prayerful friends, whom I saw regularly, and who listened beautifully. However as I was a carer, mum and worked full time, I didn't have the capacity to always share what was going on to a wider circle. And I regret if people feel I was not as forthcoming as I might have been – I was not trying to be hurtful – just to live out each day. My primary focus was to support Colin.

And so I ask for forgiveness and understanding, for my coping mechanism in an ongoing stressful situation, was largely to keep things to myself. God was the One who was my Confidant, and who gave me strength each day. Meantime I thank everyone who accompanied me in this journey, as I value all of you, whether I was sharing things in more or in less detail. Whether it was laughing or crying, your support was invaluable.

Love bears all things. (1 Corinthians 13:7)

Prayer

> Gracious God, what an amazing friend you give to us in Christ Jesus,
>
> a friend, who is closer than a brother, who lifts up my soul.
>
> Teach us all to value our friendships, to treasure times spend together, to be kind,
>
> and to connect in a rich variety of ways, to support and encourage one another, Amen

Blog 4: A Million Thank Yous

25th June 2020

On behalf of Andrew and myself, I want to thank everyone so much who attended, and showed an interest in our book launch of *Love Song for a Wounded Warrior*. We are so greatly humbled by your prayers and good wishes and comments, and are very moved by the support of so many.

The idea of this book was to honour the memory of my late husband Colin, who wanted his memories and recollections of his time in military service, especially Northern Ireland, to be published. Last night at the book launch, I read out one of his poems, and I was so heartened by people really listening to what it was about, and relating to the horror of war. Just in that one part of the meeting alone, it fulfilled so much of what we hoped for.

We were also grateful for the words of Shirley from 'Epilepsy Connections', who spoke so caringly, and with such insight as to the situation of so many people with epilepsy in Scotland, and the struggles they face. And to have Allana with us was so lovely, from the 'Coming Home Centre', who has such a passion to support veterans and their families on their return to civilian life. The work of these two charities is inspirational and they go the extra mile to help others.

We were delighted that the Moderator of the General Assembly of the Church of Scotland, Revd Dr Martin Fair could come along, and for his words of encouragement and grace. We also heard the words of Revd Dr Jock Stein, who edited and published the book, and who was such a brilliant support in bringing the book to this point.

Andrew speaking about the way his dad's disability affected him, gave very real insight into the difficulties that can be faced by children of veterans. After a time of questions and answers, the meeting came to a close, but it was such a wonderful time to hear people acknowledge Colin's story, and both he and his parents would have been so pleased.

In my end is my beginning (T.S. Eliot, *The Four Quartets*)

I was thinking of these words, and how God can bring something good even out of the most dark and difficult of circumstances, and praying that out of this book might come funds to support veteransr, and also conversation about how to better care them, and for people with epilepsy and brain damage. The conversation seems to have started already, and I hope that out of Colin's life and death, God can bring something which will bless and help others.

An enormous thank you all, for participating in this process with me, whether near or far. Our society is under such pressure just now, but anything that can help us to think about how we can support people with complex needs and difficult behaviours, is surely central to that question about what it means to love and care for some of the most vulnerable in our society. I will keep blogging, because somehow I always seem to have something to say! But just now, thank you from the bottom of our hearts.

Dear God, we give thanks for your faithfulness in difficult days,

for the support of friends and family, for moments of connection and care,

that out of despair and pain, can come possibilities of new beginnings.

Lord Jesus, bless all those today, who are veterans or veterans' families, who are carers for people with epilepsy or disabilities.

Grant them the right support, respite, wise guidance, humour and love in the midst of the challenges of every day life,

and guide and sustain all those who seek to support them, Amen.

Blog 5: Seeking Healing for Wounds

6th July 2020

> Being able to feel safe with other people is probably the single most important aspect of mental health; safe connections are fundamental to meaningful and satisfying lives.
>
> —BESSEL VAN DER KOLK

The last 10 days have been very emotional, the book launch, replying to comments, sending out books to people. I am so grateful that the book is published, and my husband's wishes honoured, and I thank people for their thoughtful insights, and encouragement. Colin would have loved that people heard his poems, and read of his experiences.

It has also been a time of pain – reliving things again, and realising that the impact of some of these things are still very much with us as a family. The memories don't leave you, but we pray that they will become less distressing, and that we learn from them, and that God uses them for good.

Some people think that for a wound to heal, it needs to be exposed to air. This is controversial, but it could be that at times exposing an emotional wound is helpful, so it doesn't fester, and that talking it through in a safe place may bring understanding and perspective. In life, we often have difficult experiences, and they can leave scars that tell their own story. God can bring healing in different ways, through being listened to, prayer, appropriate trauma therapies etc, often through connection, as Bessel's quote on the previous page indicates.

One of the books that has always spoken to my soul is Henri Nouwen's *The Wounded Healer,* and he talks about how the things that hurt us can be redeemed. He says that no one can escape being wounded, but this gives us an opportunity. Instead of our wounds being a source of shame, they can be put at the service of others – this is what it means to be a 'wounded healer'.

When we are hurting, the pain is such that we are often immobilised. We cannot see beyond it. But once the healing process starts, it often helps to find some kind of meaning in what has taken place, wherever possible. I believe that God does not want to cause us pain, but when things go wrong, he can help us find something to learn from it, even in our hurt and shame. Telling our story can be part of that healing process.

In Isaiah 53:5, it says of the suffering servant, 'By his wounds, we are healed', and as Christians we know that Jesus' death on the cross brings us cleansing, forgiveness, and healing, the possibility of new beginnings. For all those who are wounded veterans, and their families, or people struggling with disabilities or mental health issues, or people weary of lockdown, may they trust in Jesus, and find the deep healing that he can bring.

Let us pray:

> Lord Jesus, you understand the things that have hurt us and caused us pain, the memories we struggle with, the injuries we have endured, and inflicted.

In your life, you were mocked, beaten, and died on a wooden cross, yet your love shone, even then.

For all who hurt today, come along side us and bring healing grace and hope, bring healing in the way best for each individual,

so that we in turn, can provide a listening ear, prayer, and a safe space for others to feel heard and valued and loved.

Holy Spirit help us we pray, in Jesus' name, Amen.

Blog 6: Beauty Healing the Soul

11th July 2020

Beauty in unexpected places

Dear friends, what a journey we have all been on – the fears and stresses of Covid 19 and Lockdown, and the gradual release of restrictions. And as we begin to reflect on all that has happened, we are gradually realising more of the devastation that has taken place, and the impact of this time on our world, our community, and on us as individuals. The ripples are still gradually spreading outward, and the impact of the loss of freedom, employment, health and precious lives is just beginning to be felt more keenly.

Our Christian faith helps us in times of stress and exhaustion, and it seems important to ask for a summer of rest and restoration, to have time for God to repair the damage to our souls, to heal our broken hearts, to give us space to find our healing and equilibrium. Our lives have been turned upside down, and in this time of fluidity, many of us have questioned what is really a priority in our lives. It is a time of soul searching and of seeking God's guidance as to the way ahead.

My own experiences are still pretty raw, but I know that many people share these same types of difficult memories and pain, so I wanted to offer a few ways to self care over the summer months, that might help us on our journey.

God provides all we need, and he gives us nurture for our souls, as we read the bible, listen to praise music, and ask him to speak to our souls – he brings us a word in season. Worship also reminds us of the bigger eternal perspective, which helps us put our own situation into context. The joy of singing (by ourselves, and for me with no-one listening!) enables us to lose ourselves in God's love.

God inspires us in so many ways through Creation – through the grandeur of the hills, the roar of the sea, the babble of a stream – and soothes our souls.

God wants us to take care of our bodies also – these temples of the Holy Spirit – by eating healthily, taking exercise, and resting.

Sometimes sitting with a blanket, a candle and a journal, can create the space, so we can hear from the Holy Spirit, and find our healing and peace.

> He lets me rest in green meadows
>
> He leads me beside peaceful streams
>
> He renews my strength.
>
> *Psalm 23:2, NLT translation*

Let us pray

> Dear God, all wise and all knowing,
>
> Look upon your children, in our weariness and brokenness,
>
> Lord Jesus, grant us forgiveness and grace, rest and peace,
>
> so we can worship you in the beauty of your holiness,
>
> and be lost in wonder, love and praise,
>
> and know once more, that all is indeed well, Amen.

Blog 7: The Rhythm of the Sea

20th July 2020

When people feel out of kilter or worried or sad, a healing place to go is often the sea. It has so many moods, colours and tides, strengths and sounds – but somehow it can soothe the soul.

For thousands of years, the sea has had a great attraction to many. Yet the power and the dangers of the sea are many.

Vincent Van Gogh said, 'The fishermen know that the sea is dangerous and the storm terrible, but they have never found the dangers sufficient to remain on the shore.'[8]

The power of the sea is immense, and a storm can cleanse the air and bring deep peace. The sound of lapping water, the ebb and flow of the waves, can soothe the soul – it is almost as if it resets our hearts. Helen Keller said, 'I could never stay long enough on the shore. The tang of the

---

8   Van Gogh, *Ever Yours – the Essential Letters*, Yale University Press, 206.

untainted, fresh sea air, was like a cool quiet thought.'[9] The poet George Herbert said, 'He that will learn to pray, let him go to the sea.'

When we are overtired, or need refreshment for our souls, God can speak through the sea, to remind us of our smallness in his presence, to remind us of a healthier rhythm of life, or just to quieten a troubled spirit . If we have a chance this summer, may we find ourselves at the shore (even if only in memory) and find the healing touch of God.

Let us pray:

> Creator God, the source of all life and beauty, bring us to places of mesmerising beauty, that brings perspective to our sadness. Lord Jesus, speak your word of peace to troubled souls out in the storms, and may your Holy Spirit bring a refreshment and vitality to our lives, Amen.

Blog 8: Praying in Desolate Places – Finding Courage!

22nd July 2020

---

9   Helen Keller, *The Story of My Life, and Selected Letters*, Bantam Classics 53.

Holidaying in Scotland is mixture of experiences, some of colour and vibrancy, but also of mist on bleak grey landscapes.

At times, when you have got soaked yet again, you question the meaningfulness of wilderness experiences. Traipsing through the horizontal rain and squelching mud can be challenging. But then the clouds lift a little, the light changes and you find unexpected beauty that takes your breath away. It is all worthwhile.

Recently I have been reading Brene Brown's *Braving the Wilderness,* about having the courage to be your authentic self, even when it might unsettle or offend. Her insights into vulnerability and empathy and belonging are so very moving, and encourage us all to have the courage to be honest. For me, writing *Love Song for a Wounded Warrior* felt like telling our story in a wilderness of fear and potential judgement.

I was reading Maya Angelou the other day, and one thing attributed to her is this: 'There's no greater agony than having an untold story within you.' Certainly, that can feel like a festering wound. After a while, the fears around telling the story become less than the consequences of not telling it.

The wilderness is often part of a journey. For the Israelites, they were 40 years in the wilderness, learning to rely completely on God before they got to the promised land. For Jesus himself, when he was tired and burdened, he often withdrew to desolate places to pray. In these bleak landscapes, there are no distractions or places to hide – it is just us and God, and so his tender love becomes our sole focus and reality – the moment of illumination that we seek.

Whatever place we find ourselves today, even in a place of questioning and shadow, may God help us find the courage to pray and to be our true selves, ready to speak the words that are on our hearts.

Dear God, when clouds gather, we confess that we tend to like the days of sunshine more than the rain – forgive us our selfishness.

Thank you that even in the most dark dreich wildernesses, Lord Jesus, you call us not to be afraid, to surrender all that is false, and to commune more deeply with you, so that this enables us to find the courage to be both vulnerable and honest.

Holy Spirit, you transform our lives through your loving purpose and inspiration. Summon out our courage, and creativity, to be true to our calling, and to journey forward, in Jesus' name, Amen.

Blog 9: Sky – Bringing a Change of Perspective!

24th July 2020

A stunning and ever-changing expanse above

In recent days, I have been visiting Skye, and noticed the soothing rhythm of the tides, the desolation of the mountainous landscape inspiring courage, and now the ethereal beauty of the light evoking reverence. The skies here are more than awesome! (Skies on Skye seems to be a bit of play on words!)

The light on the Cuillin mountains has often been dramatic, with shades of dark and black and grey. The sea bays are adorned with purple heather and yellow seaweed. And the seas reflect the colour of the skies – from dark and moody to brilliant cobalt blue, with every combination of cloud formation drifting across the top in different layers. You can be mesmerised just watching the sky change, moment by moment.

The heavens proclaim the glory of God, the skies display his craftsmanship. Day after day they continue to speak, night after night, they make him known. They speak without sound or word, their voice is never heard. Yet their message has gone throughout the earth, and their words to all the earth.

Psalm 19:1-4, NLT version

The poet Gerald Manley Hopkins says that 'the earth is charged with the grandeur of God', and there is this sense of God's majesty and creativity being revealed through his creation.

After the confinement of lockdown, and the trauma of individual stories and difficult experiences, to see the expansive sky above, opens up our horizons, and refreshes our soul. The intricate patterns of deep colours and cloud formations inspires us to look up, to be reminded that there is so much more to life than day to day practicalities. The beauty of the sky can take our breath away, can fill us with reverent thanksgiving for all tbat is good, can remind us that God is the original and most imaginative Artist ever !

If we are worn down by cares and worries, if our life can feel a little grey, may we be inspired to look up, and be reminded of the power and glory of God, and may this give us hope.

Let us pray:

> Eternal Father, your Creation is magnificent, whether it is the vibrancy of stars in a jet black night, or white fluffy clouds on a bright blue morning.

> Lord Jesus, slow us down, and open our eyes wide, so we might notice your glory, and gain a new reverence for life.

> Holy Spirit, grant us a new perspective on our priorities and opportunities, and encourage us to be more creative in how we live each day, to relish colour and form and light. In Jesus' name, Amen.

Blog 10: Joy in the Journey

3rd August 2020

Surges of activity and then rest

Dear friends, we are all on a journey from one place to another. For some of us, as lockdown restrictions ease, we have physically travelled. For all of us, we know that we are on a spiritual journey through life, taking us from experiences in the past into whatever lies ahead. There are many stony paths, diversions, hill tops and even dead ends, sometimes we are injured *en route*, and we need so much guidance as we travel.

One of the wonderful things about God, is that he has promised to be with us. We want to learn from the past, to rejoice in the good, to learn from our mistakes, to find healing for the sadnesses, so we can continue on our journey. Often we reach a crossroads on the path, and have to work out our next step.

The famous words in Proverbs 3:5-6 say, 'Trust in the Lord with all your heart, and he will make your path straight.'

Taking time to listen to God, to pray, to study his word, to take time to reflect, so we can discern the way ahead is so vital. And it is only knowing where we have come from, that helps us work out our next steps. Being more open and honest about my life in the past has been exhausting and scary, but hopefully eventually it might be liberating. The Holy Spirit sometimes takes us through the wilderness (not our first choice of location!) yet the things we learn – our complete dependence on God for all things – couldn't be experienced any other way.

In a conversation recently, some one said that they were 'plodding' and sometimes there is a heaviness to our lives, we are just putting one foot in front of another.

A song from Michael Card encourages me; it has the following lyrics:

> There is a joy on the journey,
>
> There's a light we can love on the way.
>
> There is a wonder and wildness to life,
>
> And freedom for those who obey.

Sometimes the journey is uphill, and we are breathless and our muscles are sore. Sometimes we have to stop and rest for a while. Sometimes we have to check our compass, and go a different route. But with our Saviour with us, there is light and wonder and wildness on that journey, and paradoxically freedom from obedience. And a joy, even in the hardest of places.

Whether we are in a dark marsh, a rain soaked walk, or a mountaintop, may we somehow find joy on our journey, a thanksgiving for the process, and hope that our destination might bring better things.

Let us pray:

> Dear God, your people often set out on journeys, Abraham and Sarah, Moses, David and so many others. We too are travelling through life, and sometimes the road is clear, but other times we are disorientated and in the dark. Be our Guide, Lord Jesus, and may we have courage to follow your voice. May your Holy Spirit help us find that freedom in obedience, that brings us thanksgiving and joy, Amen.

Blog 11: A Legacy of Wonder – the Ice Cubes are Dancing!

10th August 2020

We have had a beautiful weekend – my amazing son Andrew has become 21 years old. For a mum, you wonder where all the years went – they pass so quickly in a whirl.

It has been a very emotional time. We are so sad that Colin – Andrew's dad isn't here to celebrate with us, nor Colin's parents. So much loss, and a big gaping hole in our lives. Having tried to write a little about Colin's life too, my soul is full of the things that went wrong, times of illness and irritation.

However I also wrote some personal notes about Andrew's life as he grew up, just now and again, to remember some of the details of his childhood. And at the weekend, I reread these, and it has been so healing. It reminded me of Andrew's courage, his complete independence as a small boy, his determination, his quirky sense of humour, his insights, his patience. Andrew has an amazing turn of phrase – like when he was small, and he looked at his orange juice one hot day, and said, 'the ice cubes are dancing.' Once you hear this, ice cubes are never the same again, they move and clink and dance to an unheard beat. It is seeing the wonder in the ordinary.

And so, even as I look back over the years, and grieve the losses and pain of my husband's disability, so I have been reminded of the moments of mercy and wonder in every day. I am so privileged to have a son, who has always done his own thing, and who has brought us such joy. Whether it is his love of cars and their engines, or his insights into science fiction, or his infectious enjoyment of water fights, our lives were always full.

And I think of Jesus saying of his sheep in John 10:10a: 'I have come that they might have life, and have it to the full.' Jesus gives us the gift of life, with its sorrows and splashes of light, to experience the sadness of life, and moments of connection and inspiration that are so ethereal it makes you cry.

And so today, I am full of a deep gratitude, for the vivid reminder that in the midst of uncertainty and illness, God blessed us as a family with a beautiful life together – however uproarious and chaotic it looked! And Colin's legacy lives on in Andrew's hard work, strength, loyalty, insight and humour.

May we value our children, and all our loved ones, and tell them what they mean to us, and savour every moment we have with them. May we always pray and encourage them, so that a legacy of wonder and love can be passed down.

Let us pray:

> Dear God, Creator of all things, you share with us all that you are, love, mercy, goodness and truth, forgiveness, wonder and joy – as Jesus demonstrates, life in all its fullness. Life can be bittersweet, but may your Holy Spirit keep our hearts from becoming hard, and enable us always to see the wonder around us, and to share that dance and legacy of love with others, Amen.

Blog 12: The Scream of Trauma

17th August 2020

When considering the state of the world just now, the scream of trauma seems to reverberate across every land – the child in the refugee camp, the parent unable to feed their child, the person subject to sexual violence, the individual unjustly incarcerated. For no fault of their own, often people end up caught in cross fire, suffering anguish which can damage and break a spirit. It can be so overwhelming to contemplate, and so we often switch off by not watching the news, saying that these scenes are too much to bear.

EDWARD MUNCH, THE SCREAM
(NATIONAL MUSEUM OF NORWAY)

As a Christian, I can't pretend these things are not happening, whether it is the war veteran struggling with violent memories, of the human rights lawyer in a Chinese prison, or a survivor of abuse. Some days I can't do much, others I can pray, write letters, campaign, give.

Jesus never turns his back on those who cry to him, he understands mocking, physical assault, trauma, to feel alone in the darkness. On the cross he cried: 'My God, my God, why have you forsaken me?' (Matthew 27:46). In Isaiah 42:3 the prophet says: 'A bruised reed he will not break, and a smouldering wick he will not snuff out,' and this reminds us of the tender care of God, for those who are hurting and feel bruised by life's tribulations. God has a deep concern for those who are suffering, and in anguish.

So if someone has suffered trauma and abuse, what can we do? There are many routes in different circumstances, judicially involving the police or safeguarding where appropriate, and counselling, prayer and specialist help.

Last year I had the privilege of listening to Dr Bruce Perry talking about childhood trauma, and then reading one of his books *The Boy Who was Raised as a Dog*. The book gives different case studies of traumatised children, and offers different approaches as to what helps. It is a hard but beautiful and deeply emotional read.

Dr Perry recounts true case histories of children, and tells us of the impact their trauma has had on their brain development. This in itself is such a detailed area of neuroscience, with so much to learn. And the things that can help bring healing are empathy, understanding, connectiveness, healthy relationships and love.

And so, when we think of that scream of pain echoing round the world, we pray for a powerful wave of God's love in Christ, to heal and bring forgiveness, trust and places of safety, where people can find restoration and grace. And God often uses doctors, such as Dr Perry, and so many others, to bring understanding and healing for so many. We are thankful for all who work in neuroscience and psychiatry to bring support and help to others. And we are thankful for the wider trauma therapists also, for the wisdom and insight they bring. We need to be discerning in this area, but also to be thankful for God's healing power in body, mind and soul.

Let us pray:

> Gracious God, you created this world to reflect the harmony of the trinity, but instead we fight and exploit and tear apart. Forgive us for our cruelty and greed.
>
> Lord Jesus, may there be many wise healers, who heal not just with medicine, but with prayer and empathy, understanding and love.
>
> Holy Spirit, help us not to turn away from disturbing screams, from ourselves and from others, but help us to be honest, and through tears and lament, to find our healing, Amen.

Blog 13: A Convergence of Sorrow and Love

25th August 2020

Light and shade

In life sometimes there can be the juxtaposition of too many sorrows. The loss of a loved one, of a job, of a dream, all coming at the same time. There are so many things that can cause people to mourn, not just our personal circumstances, but the loss of certainty, a wailing over injustice, a deep sorrow at the state of the world. In this time of pandemic, turbulent international politics and horrendous poverty and injustice, we have so many reasons for sorrow.

Walking in the valley of the shadow can be scary and lonely. There are so many dark places on the path, which are unexpected and unnerving. Yet it is when we are under pressure, that we call out to our Saviour, when we find out what it means to have him walk beside us on that path.

One of my favourite verses is from Isaiah 45:3, 'I will give you the treasures of darkness, riches stored in secret places'.

I often ponder what this means, but it seems to be that it is only when everything goes wrong, and you feel overwhelmed, that the beauty of Jesus' presence can be truly felt and appreciated. Somehow it is only through being in the darkness, that we find out who we really are, and the discover the blessing of God's grace to us. For he never turns his back on us, and when we are weak, he holds us up, and encourages us each step of the way.

And so there is a convergence of sorrow and love, for it us only in the deepest despair, that we experience the tender and transformative love of God, his Holy Spirit refining our characters, so the dross is burned away, and only the gold comes forth. We are changed forever, with such an overwhelming waterfall of love flowing over us, that we are cleansed and strengthened and inspired.

The cross points to this deep truth, because in this place of human cruelty and barbarism and pain, Jesus lived out the love of God, revealing concern for his followers, forgiveness for the sinner, and a trust that he could commit his spirit to his heavenly Father. The cross is the most powerful and moving expression of love, because it is when Jesus is desolate and separated from his heavenly Father, we see the extent of his self giving love for all.

This encourages our hearts, for when we are burdened looking after a loved one who is chronically unwell, or when we are struggling with pain and ill health, and life seems colourless and drab, that is when Christ's presence gives us new strength, when we feel appreciation of a random act of kindness, when we are gently drawn into an experience of love that defies all description. In the darkest moment, God can bring a revelation of his grace, which whispers to our souls a word of peace.

I feel really thankful, that even in my worst days, God was there. Even when it seemed no one understood, God listened. Even when all seemed lost, God was faithful. We are so blessed.

I remember the words of that great hymn, 'When I survey the wondrous cross' and the third verse says this: 'See from his head, his hands, his feet, sorrow and love flow mingled down; did e'er such love and sorrow meet, or thorns compose so rich a crown?'

May we pray:

> Gracious God, we give thanks that even on the most drab and empty days, in the midst of our unmittigating sorrow, you reveal to us the depth of your love in Christ, that convergence of sorrow and love on the cross, and you meet with us, and through your Holy Spirit breathe new strength and life into our souls. Your amazing love demands all we have, gladly given in love and service, and so we declare our love and devotion for you anew, Amen.

Blog 14: The Anguish of War Movies

29th August 2020

UNDER FIRE

When I first wanted to start understand my late husband Colin better, as well as listening to his military experiences, we watched some war movies together. This was to give me more insight as to what war could feel like.

Over time, we watched movies like 'Platoon', 'Full Metal Jacket', 'Apocalypse' now, 'Letters from Iwo Jima'. At the time, I felt this was really useful, helping me realise the confusion, brutality, senselessness and anguish of violence and conflict. Another film that was particularly memorable and disturbing was 'Jacob's Ladder', thinking of the delusions and sheer hell of war.

Whilst these films enabled us to talk through issues of war, justice, the horror of impossible choices, the loss of humanity involved in battle, I think they often retraumatised my husband rather than helped him. They reminded him of duty, comradery and courage, but also reinforced all the nightmares of darkness and pain and questioning.

At this point in time, I can't bear to watch any of these movies any more. They just speak to me of the senselessness and savagery of combat, which brings overwhelming sorrow and anguish. The cries of the wounded and maimed seem to echo forever in my head.

And so I look to Jesus for guidance. Our Saviour personally experienced the worst cruelty and violence of humanity, yet his love was never diminished or tarnished. He kept forgiving, was full of goodness, kept working for an eternal kingdom of truth, goodness, justice and peace.

2 THE BLOGS (JUNE 2020 – FEB 2022)

In different seasons of our lives, different things are helpful. Films, plays, books can all remind us of the moral complexities of conflict, their long lasting and often devastating impact on individuals and communities. There are theological and philosophical challenges as to what constitutes a 'just war'. Having any understanding or insight into each context, helps us pray and campaign and protest, as our conscience leads us.

I am struck by the extent to which I felt, and can still feel as if I was in some of these military conflicts with my husband, because of all the memories he shared. PTSD is not just experienced by veterans, but also often by their families. This vicarious trauma, is because of their exposure to repeated stories and re enactments of violence and suffering.

My concern therefore is that veterans and their families get the support they need to work through these traumas, and find a self worth, understanding, healing and peace. These can come through various trauma therapies, and ultimately from Jesus Christ, as our Healer and the Lover of our souls.

Meantime, we also need to find balance, by focusing on the good, the brightness of sunshine, the joy of a pet, the taste of a good meal, the encouragement and prayers of a friend, the inspiration of the Holy Spirit.

I remember the words from Philippians 4:8, where Paul writes, 'Finally dear friends, whatever is true, whatever is noble, whatever is right, whatever is pure, whatever is lovely, whatever is admirable, if anything is excellent or praiseworthy – think about such things'.

As a corollary to thinking of the darkness and barbarism of humanity, we need to remember the light and beauty and nobility, and so these words speak to my soul.

Let us pray:

> Dear Father God, you look upon us with the mercy and kindness of a beloved parent. On this earth, we fight and squabble, we often loose sight of our humanity, we use torture and violence all too easily, especially in times of conflict and war.
>
> Lord Jesus, please forgive us, heal us, restore our humanity, bless our veterans and families, and give us wisdom as to when war is ever necessary. Holy Spirit, help us to notice the good, the pure, the lovely things in our midst, and to find our peace, Amen.

Blog 15: The Banality of Evil

13th September 2020

Recently I watched the 2012 film 'Hannah Arendt'. It was a film about the political theorist covering the 1962 war crimes trial of Adolf Eichman, and one of the phrases she uses as she watches the trial is 'the banality of evil'. She is asking questions about who is responsible when things go wrong, and bureaucrats argue that they were just following orders.

It reminded me of a deeply troubling book I read many years ago, *People of the Lie* by Scott Peck. He spoke of case studies he had been involved in, where all the family members seemed 'nice' on the outside, but at times had deeply damaged others by verbal manipulations and a basic denial of their humanity. It could be subtle, but people often lied, consciously or unconsciously, and this could cause devastating harm to others.

It made me think about how trauma and harm can be not just big dramatic events, but a hundred small things. Things that can seem petty, but have a cumulative effect. When I listened to Colin talking about his days in the military, the damage was not just from the horrendous acts of violence, but also from small seemingly insignificant details, that became deeply symbolic of the emotional cost of what took place.

For Eve in the garden of Eden, we are told that she had complete freedom to do anything, except eat from the tree of the knowledge of good and evil. And the serpent knew how to tempt her, to distort what God said, and she saw the apple looked delicious. What could be the harm? Just a complete breakdown of trust.

We are all rebellious, we all make mistakes, and the logical consequence of this, is that we all contribute to the darkness in the land. Everytime we verbally put some one down, we don't challenge injustice, we collude with untruths, we are part of the problem.

Sometimes when we look at conflict and war in the world, we think it doesn't affect us, as it is geographically far away. Yet the interconnectedness of international relations, means that there is usually an element of responsibility somewhere, in terms of our history, influence, selling of weapons and financial interests. We often turn away from any responsibility to get involved, and that has consequences.

I don't want to make you feel down, but maybe we all need to reflect on our own contribution to misunderstanding, conflict and institutional evil. We need to discern when to speak out, to challenge the corporate giant, the corrupt government, to be willing to pray, to lobby, to speak. We have a responsibility to do so. Even if one situation was influenced to do something better, that would be so worthwhile.

Let us pray, and choose to act:

> Dear God, you are good and holy, and we are so rebellious and selfish, often choosing to protect ourselves, at the cost of others, choosing to be blind to the consequences.

> Lord Jesus, forgive our pride and lies and self interest, in our relationships, whether intimate or international. Open our eyes to your truth, and give us courage to act.

> Holy Spirit, keep us from temptation, help us not to compromise with the ways of the world,and help us speak out for your kingdom values. May we not collude with evil, but choose to always walk in the light, for your glory's sake, Amen.

Blog 16: When to Take Off the Mask?

19th September 2020

We have got used to wearing masks!

In these covid 19 influenced days, we are getting used to wearing masks in many situations – shops, dentists, churches etc. We know that this helps prevent the spread of the virus to others, so it is so worthwhile, even if its a bit uncomfortable.

However, in our society, it feels as if most of us are wearing a mask of some sort that prevents people seeing who we are, not just physically, but spiritually. When asked how we are, we often say that we are fine, when we feel anything but. We are often editing information to share with others, so we don't say too much.

The American pastor Rick Warren says this: 'Wearing a mask wears you out. Faking it is fatiguing. The most exhausting activity is pretending to be what you know you aren't.'

The kind of mask Rick is talking about, is a mask that we hide behind, that stops others knowing who we truly are. We often like to pretend that our life is going better than it is, that our job is great, that our relationships are harmonious, that we are in a good place. We often don't want to make ourselves look vulnerable to others by saying that we are in debt, or are wrestling with self doubt or depressed, or struggling as a parent. We don't know how people will react, and so we tend to hide.

We can all wear a mask, but at times, the weight of keeping up the pretence is overwhelming and destructive. Sometimes the secret is too big, when it comes to illness or addiction or domestic abuse. I think that some families of veterans know this pressure, because they are trying to pretend that everything is going ok, rather than admit that their much loved person has destructive behaviours. People try to be loyal, little knowing that becoming a codependent is not going to do good for anyone in the long run.

Jesus said: 'You are truly my disciples if you remain faithful to my teachings. And you will know the truth, and the truth will set you free.' (John 8:31-32)

Pretending to be what we are not, is a stressful burden. It is often driven by fear and insecurity. If I tell the truth, will people still respect me, will they still talk to me? It is such a strain to live with. The amazing thing us that God knows the truth about us, even our most dark secrets, and he still loves us. How incredible is that? And being able to be real with God in prayer, helps us to find that freedom we crave. Freedom to admit the truth, however difficult, and even to get the support that is needed.

For many people, struggling under the strain of pretending, please trust your worries to God. He will not reject you or abandoned you, rather he looks upon you with love and grace. He shows compassion on the weary and the hurting, and seeks to guide us, and to help us. God can be trusted!

I understand a little of this, as telling Colin's story has been one of the hardest thing I have ever done, and at times people don't like what I am saying. Yet being authentic, is the only way I can come to terms with all that has happened, and to seek to heal, and to find a new way forward. The truth is setting me free, although it us a gradual process, and I am so impatient.

So we might need to keep our covid preventative mask on, but to take our soul mask off. We have to ask God for wisdom, to discern if there are people we can trust to do this with. Being honest is such a relief, and helps us find our healing. My prayer is that each of us reaches out for help when we need it. May God give us courage, and bless us all with that loving friend or safe person that we can talk to.

Let us pray:

> Gracious God, you are loving, a God of integrity and grace; look upon your children with mercy, for we tie ourselves in knots with pretence and lies, and self doubt.
>
> Lord Jesus, give us courage to tell you the truth about our past, about our struggles, and to find the forgiveness and healing we seek.
>
> Holy Spirit where you dwell there is freedom. Free us, and our loved ones from lies and deception, and help us find the support that us most needed. In Jesus' name, Amen.

Blog 17: Changing Colours of Autumn

26th September 2020

This weekend, the weather has been glorious, and the colours rich and vibrant. The soft autumn sunshine, azure skies and soft clouds floating by are idyllic. The sun has been surprisingly warm, and if you find a sheltered spot, it is like being touched by the love of God.

Yet the message of all of this, is that the seasons are changing, that the leaves are starting to turn, and then to fall, sometimes gently, sometimes in a stormy frenzy of whirl.

Autumn brings hope, because it reminds us that change can be beautiful. As human beings, we often seem stuck, stuck in grief or trauma or illness. We get used to it, and forget that there is another way to live.

Jesus was always on the move, going to different places, meeting new people, praying, challenging people as to how they could follow him. He was never static. So we too are called to be open to learning, to explore our creativity, to deepen our spirituality, to be fashioned into the very image of Christ. The Holy Spirit is ever at work within us.

When we enjoy the changing autumn colours, I think God is also inviting us to change – to somehow find deeper healing from the past, and the courage to move on. This seems to be slow, painstaking work. We complain as the leaves fall, as there is so much to let go of, regrets, old patterns of thinking, difficult memories, dark hurts. Yet if the tree lies bare for a winter, by spring there is new life, new growth, new colour.

For all those entranced by the melancholy beauty of autumn, may we allow God to search our souls, guide our thoughts, to help us to choose wisely, to establish a new rhythm of life. It might be a painful transition involving reflection and self awareness, but my prayer for all of us, is that we are able to keep going forward.

Let us pray:

> Lord Jesus, we strive to go forward, to move on from the past, but unbidden memories can force their way to the surface. Cleanse us by your Holy Spirit, and give us the vision of better things that are to come, of new growth and energy. And on days when it just seems too hard, may we just rest in the warmth of your love, and find your gift of deep, healing peace in your rays of light. Thank you Father God, that we can rest with you, to marvel at your beauty, and be in communion with you, Amen.

Blog 18: Finding freedom!

10th October 2020

At this time of coronovirus and lockdown restrictions, life can seem a bit heavy. In the west of Scotland, we are not to leave our houses unless it is necessary, and it can feel a bit as if we are in prison, unable to do the things we would normally do, to meet up with friends, or go to the theatre.

Flying in the light

In comparison with many, we are so fortunate. We are not in a refugee camp in Kenya, or in prison for our faith. We have so many things to be grateful for.

I suppose this is where perspective comes in. It is so easy to focus on the things that we cannot do, and be downcast. However God calls us to focus on what is possible, and the choices we can make.

For people who are carers though, I think this is a particularly tough season. Many support services have been cut, day centres and respite opportunities are often closed or limited. Caring for a loved one with mental health issue, a chronic condition or a disability, can be exhausting at the best of times, a 24 hour a day job. Listening in the night to meet the needs of some one who is ill, or might wander, means that feeling of never being able to relax for a second.

When I was looking after Colin, I could never anticipate his needs, or when I should be involved. He was proud and independent – he often didn't want help. He resented it. Yet on occasion, intervention seemed the lesser of two evils. It is so hard as a spouse, to deliver person centred care, and to ensure dignity. For many carers, your anticipation of risk, means you can't rest, because you are seeking to keep everyone safe.

If we are feeling trapped, whether because of personal circumstances or covid restrictions, the Christian faith can make such a difference. There is a beautiful verse: 'Where the spirit of the Lord is, there is freedom.' (2 Corinthians 3:17)

We are reminded that God releases us from our chains, he heals the broken hearted, he puts the lonely in families, he lifts up those who are down. He gives strength, insight and patience when it is needed. God is so tender hearted towards his children – he sees our struggles, and comes alongside us, to release us from what binds us, and to set us free. Our spirits can dance and soar, even in the midst of burdens and cares.

And so, dear friend, whatever might be weighing on your spirit, I pray that you can find freedom in the Holy Spirit of God, who cleanses and heals us, and inspires us and brings life.

Let us pray:

> Lord God, at times our burdens are so heavy, we feel weighed down and trapped. But Lord Jesus, you shine your light into our darkness. You forgive our shortcomings, you open our eyes to the beautiful, the small acts of kindness.

> Holy Spirit of God, bring us to a place of freedom, where we can soar like the eagle, and enjoy the exhilaration of the fresh air and the warmth of the sunshine. May we always know an inner freedom, that enables us to be, and to have space and identity. Help us to appreciate and explore this freedom, Amen.

Blog 19: I'll Walk You to your Car, Lass

19th October 2022

Civility in the city

Anniversaries are such strange things. You think you are prepared, but you seldom are. This month is the first anniversary of my father-in-law's death, and it feels really emotional. He lived a long and full life, and he accomplished amazing things, but I still feel so very tearful at his death.

I used to visit him and his wife on a Sunday evening, and they always made us a meal, even when that should have been the last thing in the world they should have been thinking about. My mother-in-law would make a

Sunday roast dinner for us, and took great pride in getting all the details right. How she cooked in that little scullery kitchen I will never know!

And then at the end of the evening, Tom would say to me, 'I'll walk you to your car, lass'. Every time he said this, I would just be blown away. It was an old fashioned courtesy, offered as if it was so self evident that this was the only possible thing to do. They lived in the top flat, parking on the street was often difficult, and do with my parking skills, my car was often far away. But still he pulled on his cap and jacket, and would accompany me down the stairs. He would wave me out of my parking place, stopping the other traffic, just to make sure I got home ok.

That weekly courtesy was one of many, and just spoke of his kindness and manners. Even when he was less well, it took me all my time to stop him escorting me down the stairs, even when I protested that it was raining, and I didn't want him to get wet.

Sometimes it is these little things that are so moving, so symbolic of his life, his thoughtfulness and humility and self-effacing nature. Yet he also held strong views on politics, art and culture. He was incredibly witty, loved conversation and was stimulating company at dinner. He was an artist, with an independent vision and style. He was a brilliant husband, father-in-law, dad and grandpa. So sorely missed.

May we never take our loved ones for granted. May we take time to remember them, all the memories, good and bad, funny and poignant. May we have space to speak of them fondly, and to laugh and to reminisce. Every day is so precious.

In Psalm 90 verse 12, the psalmist says, 'Teach us to number our days, that we may gain a wisdom of the heart.'

Appreciating what we have, is just so vital, giving us thankful hearts, and puts all things in perspective.

> Gracious God, our times are in your hands, and we are so grateful for all who have gone before us, who have shared their lives with us, who inspired us, and loved us. Lord Jesus, help us treasure all the ways you have blessed us, all the people who have shown us kindness. Holy Spirit, may the example of those who have gone before us, inspire us to live each day for good, that we may love and show compassion and thoughtfulness to others, and to seek to make this world a better place. Amen.

Blog 20: Honouring a Legacy?

31st October 2020

This week, one of our very long standing church members died, and had a funeral that celebrated her long and incredibly full life. It was very moving, to reflect on all that she did, and she was described as a pioneer of her time. One of our challenges as a church, is how we live up to her legacy.

This started me thinking about what we leave behind us. None of us knows the number of our days, so how do we make them count?

I found a quotation from the 4th century Greek statesman Pericles: 'What you leave behind is not what is engraved in stone monuments, but what is woven into the life of others.'

I started writing because I wanted to honour my late husband's life. Somehow, telling his story, helps us as a family, to find meaning in what has taken place, and to honour his legacy.

Part of this is shaped by a desire to raise the profile of the need for more effective care for veterans. The damaging nature of the long term emotional, spiritual and physical injuries after serving in armed conflicts, cannot be over-estimated. And the impact on relationships and families can be immensely destructive.

It also feels important to raise awareness of the need for more research into epilepsy, and the exploration of possible new treatments. If someone's seizures are well controlled by medication that is great, but if their epilepsy is intractable, life is challenging.

To honour Colin's legacy, in the midst of these two strands, I also want to give thanks for people who have supported and prayed with us. God gave us kind people around us, guided our path, and sustained us on the darkest days, granting us all we needed.

And so Colin's legacy is that even in the midst of trauma and disability, we are not to give up, that God gives us strength each day, leads us to helpful people, enables us to laugh, helps us find an internal resilience that we did not know we had. Every day of life is precious. God gives our lives a quality of love and grace that is life changing.

At times, I question writing about all this, because it makes you so vulnerable. But this feel like our purpose to try to encourage others,, and the best way I can honour Colin, so I pray for strength to do so, especially in these days leading up to Remembrance.

In Ephesians 5:2 it says: 'Live a life of love, love others as Christ loved us.'

The legacy of Christ, is indeed love, and so sharing that love, truth and grace with others, is our greatest calling.

Let us pray:

> Gracious God, forgive us that we often don't think what our spiritual legacy is to the next generation. Lord Jesus, may we be inspired by generations of Christian people, who have faithfully and creatively followed you. May our life's purpose be to honour the legacy of all who have gone before, and may your Holy Spirit guide us as to what to do, as we seek to pass on your life changing and transformative love and truth to others, Amen.

Blog 21: Remembrance – Lamentation and Brutality

7th or 14th November

Remembrance Day is one of the hardest of the year, thinking of all who have served, been injured and died in conflict and war. We think of the first world war 1914-18 and the second world war 1939-45. But we also think of more recent conflicts and wars, Northern Ireland, Afghanistan, Iraq.

Many of us have relatives that have fought and died, and we seek to honour their memory. But the sad fact is that many veterans who come home, have PTSD and mental health problems which can become overwhelming, and which leaves them homeless on the streets of our cities. We see them every day.

War horse

The sheer brutality and violence of war is haunting and visceral. Whether it is in the muddy trenches of Flanders, or the streets of Belfast, at Dunkirk or the opium fields of Afghanistan, shooting, bombs and explosions maim, wound and kill.

We often see such conflict expressed in film, and I remember especially seeing the film 'War Horse'. Seeing that horse entangled in the barbed wire, the barbs getting deeper into its flesh the more it struggled, and its cry of distress and pain, somehow embodies for me the cry of all who suffer the long term effects of violence and war.

The horse entangled in the wire on the battle field, reminds me of Jesus on the cross, innocent yet suffering such great pain. Jesus had done nothing wrong, but he suffered because of the guilt and violence of humanity, paying the price for our greed and selfishness, so we could be cleansed and forgiven.

When I think of my late husband Colin Gardner, and his struggles as a veteran having come home from mitary service, I think of his pride in his service, but also his colossal frustration with his disability, his perpetual recounting of traumatic experiences and his feeling that nothing else in his life could ever mean as much as his military memories. His pain, physical and emotional were enormous. This time of year and the 5th November and all the noises of the fireworks made him want to dive for cover, and to draw his gun, and retraumatised him.

The death of Jesus Christ, reminds us that on the cross, love ultimately wins, transcending hatred and cruelty, bringing forgiveness for all who seek peace. We learn even from the most horrendous pain and brutality, and find renewed purpose in working for a better world, a kingdom of justice and peace.

In this season of Remembrance, we remember all who gave their lives in conflict and war. We also give thanks for all who served, and returned, but whose experiences maimed and scarred them for life. We lament on their behalf and pray for them and for their families. May God bring to them the healing and peace they seek.

Jesus' words from John 15:13 – 'Greater love has no one than this, to lay down his life for his friends.'

Let us pray:

> Gracious Father, eternal God of hope and peace, we cry to you to have mercy upon us, for our world continues to be a place of conflict and dispute, of greed and violence. Lord Jesus Christ, you died alone on a cross, because of the greed and selfishness of our race, to be the perfect sacrifice to bring redemption and forgiveness for all. Holy Spirit, cleanse us from our pride and wilfulness, heal us from our wounds, help us to support and pray for all who struggle with the nightmares and brutality of war, and help us find new strength and peace, so that we can build for the future, Amen.

Blog 22 Longing for Shalom

21st November 2020

A quest for peace

War and conflict are greatly reflected upon, at this time of year. We have thought of legacies, lamentation, and now we seek to explore our longings. Out of a November remembering the horrors and vicissitudes of war, so now we plead for God to bring some good purpose out of all this.

Having thought of shell-shocked soldiers in the deep mud of the trenches of the first world war, and the bombings of the Atlantic convoys in the second world war, of the IEDs of more recent conflicts, the trauma and inhumanity of war experiences, broken bodies and spirits, are all too clear. The cost of conflict in human lives is incalculable.

Yet this is not the end of the story, because exposure to these military stories and experiences, reminds us of our purpose as human beings, our deep yearning for shalom, for healing and goodness and forgiveness and love and peace.

I was reminded of the biblical vision of of a peaceful Kingdom in Isaiah 11:6: 'In that day the wolf and the lamb will live together, the leopard will lie down with the lamb, the calf and the yearling will be safe with the lion, and a little child will lead them all.'

Desmond Tutu describes the fullness of biblical shalom: 'God's shalom, peace, involves righteousness, justice, wholesomeness, fullness of life, participation in decision making, goodness, laughter, joy, compassion, sharing and reconciliation.' In some ways, it seems like a long list of qualities, but shalom is just such a beautiful deep peace, the very presence of God – so it needs all these words and more just to catch a glimpse of it.

We have a deep yearning for a peaceful world, of justice and reconciliation and love. And the reason we have that, is because we have seen the alternative – a world where the loudest voice seems to win, where bullies get their own way, where lies prevail over truth, where mistrust and violence and conflict have become the norm. And the hurt and pain and tears are flowing in all nations and continents.

So let's not just accept this as ok. Let's not just put up with violence or abuse or exploitation. Let's not say that the lives of children, or people with different views are lesser in some way. Let's not say that where there is a dispute, that fighting and guns are the best way to resolve this. Have we learned nothing?

So may God give us a pure heart, to hear his voice. We need discernment, to be as wise as serpents and as innocent as doves. We need the Holy Spirit of God to help us on our narrow path, and it is not easy.

Even if we resolve to do one thing, to pray for peace, to give to charity, to not escalate a dispute, to support a veteran, to breathe before we speak – if everyone did these things, it would make such a difference. And because the task is great, may we not put it off, but have our inner compass always pointing to true North, to the larger purposes of God, for shalom for his people, for the world.

It is sometimes only when you have been through hard times, that you realise what is important in life. So out of the horror and brutality of conflict, may we yearn for something better, and resolve to work for *shalom* in our lives and world, Amen

Let us pray:

> Gracious God, Maker of the universe, you look upon our world, which you made to be so harmonious and beautiful, and you see the damage that our greed and selfishness has brought. Lord Jesus, have mercy upon us, and forgive us for our vindictiveness and struggles for status and power. Holy Spirit, humble us to seek the wellbeing of others before ourselves, to yearn for a true *shalom*, and to be channels of your peace, Amen.

Blog 23: The Significance of Doors

28th November 202

Doors opening and closing

Our beautiful dog Gabriel is so clever that he can work the door handle to the kitchen, so he could get into the fridge – his favourite place! He looks so very pleased when he manages this.

A great strategy to deal with this, was to replace the handle with a door knob, so the dog can't work it. This is an excellent solution, except sometimes I can't turn it either, and then we are both locked out of the kitchen!

This started me reflecting on the importance of doors. Sometimes we try a door, and it just won't open. It might lead to a geographical location, but sometimes to a new experience or spiritual journey. We pray, we bargain, we plead, but the door will not budge.

At other times, doors open that we hadn't even known existed, and we are amazed and bemused. Is this a door we are meant to be going through? We pray for the guidance of God to show us. A door might open easily, but this doesn't mean it is the right one.

We know from Ecclesiastes that there is a season for everything under the sun, but the transition between seasons can be messy and poorly defined. Knowing the direction of our calling, and our life is not easy to discern.

There is a song by the band 'King and Country' called 'Pushing on a pull door'. It is such a relatable song, because it is all about making plans, and thinking you know what might happen, and then everything goes upside down, and you realise that you have been pushing on a door that won't open in the way you thought. All that energy, until you learn to see things through God's eyes, and that you need to change your approach.

In this season leading up to Advent, we had plans for Christmas, and what this time might look like, but our plans have had to change dramatically. In these days of trying to keep everyone safe from the virus, we seem to be revising all our decisions daily, and it is exhausting. Do we see that person, can we travel there, should we self isolate, just in case? How do we keep people safe, but also help them to know they are remembered and loved?

Whatever our decisions, about Christmas arrangements, or our path through life, may God guide us on his path, and may we be quiet enough to listen to hear his voice speaking to us. May Jesus show us the right door to go through, and his Holy Spirit guide our steps.

> Trust in the Lord with all your heart, and lean not on your own understanding. In all your ways acknowledge him, and he will make your path straight. (Proverbs 3:5-6)

May we pray:

> Gracious God, we start off on our journey, thinking we know the doors to open, but finding that the door will not budge, and we get frustrated and bewildered. We do not know where to turn. Lord Jesus, on the road to the cross, the path was often difficult, with unexpected turns. Help us to know this can be true for us too. Please travel with us, give us courage, and through your Holy Spirit guide our footsteps, and bring us to the place of your choosing, to a place of healing love, obedience and peace. In your name, Amen.

Blog 24: Coming Home at Christmas?

5th December 2020

This is a photo of our wonderful dog Gabriel welcoming me home. Yes, he is in fact standing on the dining room table. Yes, I had only been to the bin. But there he is at the window, welcoming me back to the house, with excitement and enthusiasm!

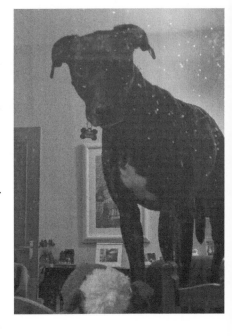

We have an image, about what it is like to be welcomed back home. It is a bit like the movie images, of a harmonious family sitting round the dinner table, synchronising forkfuls of delicious food, with a place setting with your name on it. But it is seldom exactly like this.

This year, we are all so conscious that we can meet up with a few loved ones at Christmas, under the new regulations. But it is so hard. Many people are opting not to visit, as they think this is the best way to keep loved ones safe. Others are travelling or planning, but are worried as to who to invite or not, and how that might be received. There are strained relationships and worries as to what to do. It is so complex, as to what to do for the best.

When we celebrate Christmas, we remember that we are celebrating the birth of our Saviour Jesus Christ. His birth brings Hope, Love, Salvation, Forgiveness, Joy. It is a beautiful time, whether we celebrate it alone or with others.

And if we are celebrating alone, for whatever reason, we remember the story of the Prodigal Son. He was far from home, he turned away from his family and went and did his own thing. But when he decided to go home, his Father was watching for him, and celebrated with the best robe and a feast of celebration, for the one who was lost was found.

This reminds us, that actually we are never by ourselves, for God welcomes us into his presence with a tender love and care. And this Christmas, my prayer is that every person will know that message of grace and love, wherever they may be.

There is a beautiful song called 'You came running' by Laura Story which reminds us that in Luke 15:20 it says: 'While he was still a long way off, his Father saw him, and was filled with compassion for him; he ran to his son, threw his arms around him and kissed him.' The Father sees his children, and he runs to welcome us. What extraordinary grace and undeserved love. When we are with God, we are always spiritually home.

Let us pray:

> Gracious Father, when we feel lost or alone, thank you that you are looking out for us, and long to welcome us back home. Lord Jesus, Saviour of the world, you came as the word made flesh, to open up the door to eternal life, to all who place their trust in you. Holy Spirit, prompt us to keep returning to you, to know that you never turn us away, and that we can be reconciled with our God. In the midst of disrupted plans, and empty places this Christmas, may we know how much we are loved by you, and find peace, Amen.

Blog 25: Unexpected Angels in our Midst, even Gabriel!

19th December 2020

Everyone has their own favourite film at Christmas, from 'Elf', 'Love Actually' to 'It's a Wonderful Life'. There are many films to choose from, and it seems important to enjoy them, especially with the latest lockdown restrictions announced today. People are so worried about the virus, disappointed about their plans to see loved ones which have now been cancelled, concerned about loved ones unwell or having the virus. We need some escapism, to help us to cope.

'It's a Wonderful Life' is particularly popular, as it reminds us that when we are questioning what our life is all about, maybe God has used us to accomplish more than we know. Clarence the angel is maybe not what we imagine angels to be like, but he appears just at the right time to save a life.

There are so many angelic appearances in the bible, and in the Christmas story, Gabriel the angel speaking to Zechariah in the temple, to Mary in the house, to Joseph in a dream. Angels are described as heavenly messengers that stand in the very presence of God. They do the bidding of God, answering prayer, intervening in situations, revealing God's will.

A Christmassy Gabriel

Especially in these days of difficult death statistics, restrictions and isolation, we pray for God to send His angels into this world – to remind the lonely person that they are not alone, to visit the despairing person in a hospital bed or prison cell, to remind that bereaved person or traumatised child that God wants to comfort them.

On the hillside, the angels praised God amongst the shepherds, and brought news of great joy for all people, for a Saviour was born to bring glory to God, and peace on earth. The purity of angels praising God must have been inspirational.

I believe that God still sends divine messengers to this earth, to encourage, to guide the lost, to be with the dying. Sometimes God might choose the most unlikely people to fulfil his purposes, unexpected angels are all around. And this brings us hope.

We know that in the new year, the various vaccines will be rolled out, and that this will make a difference. We know that these restrictions will not last forever. We know that the number of people ill with the virus will gradually lessen. There is much to be hopeful about.

Right now, as we look at the dark nights, and the rain drops rolling down the window pane, it is easy to feel down. May we know that God has not deserted his people, and that the angels still sing. May we notice the angels in our midst, the prayers said, the acts of kindness around, and may this strengthen us, and remind us that there are better days to come.

May we pray:

> Eternal Father, news of a new more spreadable variant of the virus is hard to hear, and the new restrictions have curtailed so many plans to meet up at Christmas. Help us to remember that the first Christmas was tough too, a long journey, a birth of a child in less than ideal circumstances. Yet God provided for the holy family, and he provides for us today. Holy Spirit, help us notice the angels in our midst, the heavenly singing, the prayer, the acts of kindness. And may we find peace, trusting in you, Amen.

Blog 26: Courage to Cross Thresholds

29th December 2020

We are heading towards the end of 2020, a threshold between the present and the future. In celtic spirituality, thresholds are often equated to 'thin places' – places where the divine is more readily experienced. It can be a spiritual place of suffering or loss, where the usual material certainties have lost their attractiveness, and we learn to rely on Christ, as our strength in our weakness and confusion.

2020 has been a year of such darkness and suffering – so many dying from the virus, people with long term effects of covid 19, loved ones unable to see each other, even in end of life situations. So much weeping.

I think of all those I have lost this year, personally and in the church family, and it is so hard to take in. All the people that I don't get to speak to again, at least in this life. I miss them.

Yet in 2020, I have also had cause to be grateful. I have listened to friends heroically looking after loved ones in impossible situations, people showing great kindness above and beyond the call of duty, prayer warriors, and encouragers and those who have sacrificially served others. It has been humbling.

I am also so deeply grateful to God, for enabling me to publish *Love song for a Wounded Warrior* this year, a tribute to my late husband – his life as a veteran, and his struggles with his subsequent medical condition. This time last year, it seemed like an impossibility: I was editing and rewriting drafts, and questioning why I would even think about doing this.

But God opened the door, and held it open so I could walk though. I faced delays and setbacks and struggles, but I felt a sense of call to honour my husband's memory, and God enabled me to do this, and I am still amazed that it actually happened. I am grateful that your donations too, have been a blessing to the 'Coming Home Centre', and to 'Epilepsy Connections'. Thank you.

I still don't know where God is leading me. I have been so encouraged by people's insights and prayers, and telling our story has been the right thing to do. It has also been costly. I feel called to continue to explore ways of finding healing for people who have experienced complex trauma, but I need courage and wisdom.

For just now, I am humbled that God has given me courage to write, to try to express what is going on my heart. All I can do, is to continue to share the themes that I struggle with, in the hope that it will help another human being, to be honest about the rubbish in our lives, to seek prayer and healing and support.

At this juncture between the old and new, I am grateful that God helped me find my voice. Thankyou too for reading this blog. I seek to be faithful to Christ, and to continue to seek supportive communities for people to find healing and hope. For we are never by ourselves, and God is always here. What an encouragement.

Let us pray:

> Lord Jesus, the pain, sorrow and brokenness of 2020 is almost too much to bear. Yet in the midst of the darkness and despair, you shine the light of your presence, a lamp to my feet, and a light for my path. Guide us all by your Holy Spirit, through the door of your choosing, and the new life beyond. Grant us hope for the new journey ahead, to put one foot in front of another, and help us to follow your healing calling, wherever it may lead, Amen.

Blog 27: One Step at a Time

9th January 2021

Beauty all around

I have discovered that I am not a very patient person. Some people will not be surprised to hear this. I often have ideas, a plan, and can't wait to put it all into practise. I am enthusiastic!

God often challenges my plans however. I often need to rethink, to pray, to ponder, to consider what to do, and what is true to my identity as a child of God.

Over Christmas, I had covid 19. I tested positive, I talked to track and trace, I self isolated for 10 days along with my son. I am so fortunate it wasn't worse, it was just like a bad flu, headaches, feeling achy, a lack of taste and smell, a cough, fatigue etc. It was very unpleasant, and lasted just over a week, until the symptoms started to lessen. I was relieved that it didn't get worse, and as far as I know, that I didn't give it to anyone else. I took all the precautions, I used my mask and anti bacterial stuff, and I am grateful that I am here. I so pray for others who have it, that they heal and have no complications.

I am so very thankful, but I do have low energy. I know I need to rest until I feel better. I am doing the essentials at work, and trying to self care. I am learning so much, for even a walk in the park leaves me exhausted, so I need to only do a few things each day. Things I took for granted are not available to me right now.

And so I need to learn to be patient, to take one step at a time. I need to acknowledge that I rely on God completely, to give me energy, to guide my path, or even allow me just to rest. Resting can be restorative and peaceful, as long as I allow myself not to feel guilty over what I cannot do.

I remember the words of Psalm 40: 'I waited patiently on the Lord, he turned to me and heard my cry.'

I need to pray, rest, and at the right time, take a wee step forward, and then rest. I am blessed with lovely supportive, prayerful family and friends, with my encouraging dog, with food and water and a warm place to live. I try to use this time to dream, and read and listen to inspirational music. I seek to develop a more thankful heart, and to notice the beauty all around, and for God to teach me to be more patient.

Let us pray:

> Gracious Father, we cry to you for all who are unwell this day, with covid 19, with cancer or other conditions, chronic and acute. Lord Jesus, we thank you for our incredible paramedics and health care teams, doing an amazing job in hospitals and GP practices around the country. Please bless them, give them wisdom and stamina, to care for those who are sick and dying, and for their relatives. For those who are recuperating, please help them to pace themselves, to rest, to breath, to self care. Holy Spirit of God, thank you for the power of prayer. May we pray for one another, to show kindness, to provide practical help, to get prescriptions or shopping. We thank you for vaccination programmes, and pray that they would protect the most vulnerable. Help us all to be patient, as we seek to keep well, and to make good choices that keep others safe. May we be patient just a bit longer, God, as we watch and pray, for we ask it in your Son's precious name. Hear our cry we pray, Amen.

Blog 28: Healing of Identity!

16th January 2021

Discovering our true self

I had a birthday this week, a lockdown birthday, which I guess has become quite distinctive. They are characterised by not being able to meet all the people you would like to, and a sense of poignancy as a result. We are all grateful to be alive, and we know keeping the rules keep people safe, so that is a small sacrifice to make. But it still feels very different.

I have been very blessed however, because there are so many ways of keeping in touch with people. And this year, it has been wonderful to be in contact in different ways with people. And actually co-writing *Love Song for a Wounded Warrior* has been part of that process, because I have been able to reconnect with lovely people I had lost touch with, or not spoken to properly for years. It has been healing to explore shared memories of different adventures that we experienced in the past.

And so, one of the things that seems to be happening in my soul, is a healing of identity. It has been healing to connect with people, and hear their stories. It has also been amazing to remember parts of my life that were at the circumference of my memory, and to bring them back into the middle.

And this has been so significant because I think when I was a carer, I completely lost sight of who I was. Just dealing with the day to day stresses and medical needs of Colin, working full time, and being a mum, meant that I didn't gave much space to exist, to make a decision, to know that I had choices. I wonder how many other carers are like this, where your identity gets completely eroded in caring for someone else. I am not complaining, that was what seemed best, to fulfil all the roles I had, to love unconditionally. However now I look back, I recognise that part of myself died. Now I am beginning to realise that I need to ask God to bring possibilities of renewal and resurrection.

Knowing who you are is a profound question. It changes and evolves over time. I love the Ignatian concept that becoming your best self is to be fully alive, the one that God has fashioned us to be. The quest is how to rediscover this, to ask God to put the fragments back together in some form of wholeness.

Many verses remind us of our identity with God, 'You are all children of God through faith in Christ Jesus.' (Galatians 3:26) We are beloved children of God, which is breath taking. A song by Jason Gray 'Remind me who I am' also speaks of the rediscovery of identity, of love and purpose. It is an important quest for each of us, especially if we might have lost our way through the pressures of life.

Let us pray:

> Gracious God, sometimes our lives seem full of jagged pieces, bits of a mosaic but with no discernible pattern. We repress painful memories, we get overwhelmed by trauma and weariness, and we feel lost and broken. In the messiness, you come to us Lord Jesus, to forgive, to hold and heal, and to remind us who we are. We thank you that we can trust you. Please bless all those who care for others, may they be supported by kindness and support and respite. Holy Spirit, recreate our identity, as your precious children, and give us courage to explore our freedom our gifts, our path forward, in Jesus' name, Amen.

Blog 29: Peace Beyond Understanding

25th January 2021

Deep rest

There are so many sad and disturbing things going on in the world just now, it can be hard to be still. There is too much to make our minds race, and to disturb our equilibrium. The number of people unwell, especially ill with covid 19 at home and in hospital is difficult to comprehend, and the consequent human misery and loss that is resulting for so many families.

In the midst of all this, it is hard to know how best to pray, I pray for the virus not to spread more, and for healing of those who are sick. But I also want to pray for peace for those who are critically ill.

I am so fortunate, as I am relatively healthy, but in times when I have been unwell, I can remember my body feeling so busy fighting infection, that my mind felt very far from reality, as if everything in the world was so far away, I was actually very peaceful. Ironically it felt like quite a safe place to be, where nothing bothers you, because you are not really thinking. You can hear people and respond in your soul, but not necessarily physically.

I was watching a YouTube clip of Joni Eareckson Tada the other day, a woman who recently had covid 19. It is quite a challenging, direct and emotional video, so watch it only if you feel able – a summary is below – https://www.youtube.com/watch?v=squAX6lV2Aw

Joni is quadriplegic, so when she got her diagnosis of covid 19, she thought she would die. She was in hospital, fighting to breathe, when she felt a deep trust in Jesus, and an odd calmness – she knew that whether she lived or died, she was with God, that she was resting in the shadow of the Almighty. And she was at peace. She wants everyone to share this peace of Christ, which is why she shares her experience.

People have different experiences and spiritual understandings, but that resting in the Almighty, that deep peace and trust is surely something that we want people to have. So they are not worried or anxious or fearful, but rather completely at rest.

Paul encourages the Christians in Philippi to trust God, to present their requests to him, and then he says 'and the peace of God, which passes all human understanding, will guard your hearts and your minds in Christ Jesus.' (Philippians 4:7)

When I feel worried or uncertain, I know I can trust Jesus, and he often shares that sense of peace with me. To be honest, there are still times when I still struggle or am restless. But God wants to bless us with his peace, and that is the gift he longs to share.

May we pray:

> Lord Jesus Christ, our hearts break over the number of people unwell and dying because of covid 19. We give thanks for all the paramedics and medical staff working with patients, especially in ICU wards, for their medical care and kindness to their patients and their families. Please bless them all, and especially those that are critically ill. May your Holy Spirit bring to them, that deep peace that passes all understanding, and may they know that whatever happens, that they can find safety in your loving hands, Amen.

Blog 30: The Joy of Photographs!

30th January 2021

Light and space

Lockdown seems to be lasting a long time – what an understatement this is! We know it is needed, to get the rates of virus transmission down, but it seems a bit endless, well actually completely endless.

A time of hibernation – when we are in a dormant state, everything seems slowed down, and going out to walk in the cold and rain can lose its appeal. It would be easy to feel a little down.

I am so impressed by people who have taken up knitting, done an on line course and learned a new language in lockdown! Such amazing self discipline and focus are needed.

One thing that can be remarkably beneficial, is to open up some old photo albums. Electronically stored photos are good too, but don't quite have the same feel. Every time you turn the page, you find a plethora of experiences, journeys and memories. They are mixed of course, sometimes people look a bit grumpy, and other times a moment of pure joy is captured – a night out with friends, a family holiday, an unexpected fun day out. Looking through photos, I am reminded of birthday meals, talking with dolphins, that trip to Moscow, swimming at Florida beaches, sunsets in Cyprus. I am reminded of all the ways that I am blessed.

I would encourage everyone to look at old photos. They remind us of family and friends, times of being together. They remind us of places we have traveled too, and the experience of different cultures and landscapes. They remind us of the richness of the lives that we have led.

God has blessed us, he watches over us in days of heartache, he gives us days of song, he inspires us with his word, he reminds us of beauty even out of ashes. We just need a little reminding at times.

'I will praise you, O Lord, with all of my heart' (Psalm 9:1)

Dear God, in lockdown, we often live much of our life within four walls, which can seem pretty claustrophobic. We cry to you to help us, when we feel hemmed in, and ask that you remind us of the freedom of your Holy Spirit. Lord Jesus, forgive us that we have short memories of the joys of past days. Give us patience, thankful hearts, and a desire to connect and bless others in safe but thoughtful ways. Thank you that your love is never restricted, but is unlimited at reaching each one of us, wherever we are, Amen.

Blog 31: It's OK to Slow Down!

6th February 2021

Appreciating slowness!

We seem to be pre-programmed to rush and be busy. We accept it as the norm, and if you ask someone how they are, and they say they are not doing much, you tend to wonder what that might mean.

Well that was true before the pandemic! For key workers, their lives are still as busy as ever. For others, people are so restricted in not meeting people or going anywhere, that response 'I'm not doing anything much' has become more common. It is often said with a mournful face, for after living under so many restrictions for so long, there is a feeling of claustrophobia at the moment. As some one said on the phone the other day, 'the days can be monotonous'.

A few years ago, I encountered a book *In Praise of Slow* by Carl Honore. The author is pleading with people not to live such hectic, busy lives, and instead to slow down, to take your time and appreciate things more. He talks of things like slow eating, working less hard, and generally appreciating ' the wisdom of slowness' – a phrase from Miles Kundera.

This line of thinking is really very liberating, for it reminds us that actually slowing down for a while can be beneficial for body and soul. If we reframe lockdown, so instead of feeling like being in prison, it is a time to reflect, and to appreciate life more, then that would be a blessing. Then it can become a sacred time, to learn to enjoy nature, to re engage with art and literature, to be more creative, and to be content in our own company. This will give us a new outlook too, when the restrictions will begin to lift, and encourage a new balance between quiet and busy.

It is never as easy as that, of course, for we are experiencing a collective mourning, which can feel crushing – so many deaths, so much illness and trauma. We need to use the quiet spaces to pray, and to give others a safe place to process and heal. It looks like this could take generations.

We remember the words from Ecclesiastes chapter 3, 'There is a time for everything under the sun.' Instead of the temptation to rush into things, may we learn to be more contemplative, to take our time, to listen to God, before we take action. Even when restrictions lessen, we might well choose to live more gratitude filled lives, with more quiet moments. This could be a pivotal decision, to help us find a healthier rhythm for our lives.

Let us pray:

> Gracious Father, we are so grateful for this extraordinary planet to live on, for the beauty and inspiration all around us. Forgive us that at times we move so quickly, that we are oblivious to the breathtaking wonder of creation, art, music and literature. Forgive us that we don't see the forgiveness and mercy of Jesus Christ, or take time to experience what it means to follow your teaching, and live in your love. Holy Spirit, help us to take this opportunity to appreciate going more slowly, and learning to notice and cherish what is truly of value in life, to love and be loved and be a blessing to others, for Jesus' sake, Amen.

Blog 32: Building Bridges not Walls

13th February 2021

A beautiful bridge

I have so enjoyed walking in the snow this week, noticing birds and squirrels and foxes. The park has been an extraordinary place of crisp snow, exquisite swirly patterns on bark, soft sunrises and a frozen pond. And every time I walk round, I pass a gorgeous wrought iron bridge, joining the land with a small island in the middle.

It has caused me to reflect on the importance of bridges in our society today. People seem to be so polarised in their opinions, whether about independence, the effects of Brexit, or about the best choices in a pandemic. Everyone seems to have a view, and they often seem to be strongly held, and loudly articulated. And people are so busy speaking, there seems little room to listen.

Listening is underrated however. Listening attentively to another human being can lead to new understanding and a fresh perspective. At the end of the time, people might still have different views, but someone perceived as an enemy could have become a friend. Listening helps to remove walls of division and hatred, brick by brick, and allow bridges to be built in their place.

In the book of James chapter one verse 19b it says: 'Everyone should be quick to listen, and slow to speak.'

The transformative impact of this teaching, if applied in our world, would be powerful. Before we spout forth, we should check our sources, listen carefully, and ask God what we should say. The checklist, 'Is it true, is it necessary, is it kind?' is a wise one to consult, before we even consider speaking. We all regret saying hasty words that have given offence to others.

In the New Testament, one of the great listeners is Barnabas – 'son of encouragement'. He was one of those people who listened to God, who saw beyond the superficial, and brought people together. An example of this is in Acts chapter 9, where Saul has had his conversion experience on the Damascus road, but when Saul got to Jerusalem, the Christian community were suspicious about the genuineness of his conversion, and wondered if he was trying to trick them. It was Barnabas who spoke for Saul, and told of his story, so bonds of trust could be built, and Saul, or Paul as he became known, was welcomed into the Christian community, and went on to become one of their most fervent leaders and letter writers. If Barnabas had not intervened, then we might never have heard of Paul!

And so in today's age, let's not be part of the vitriolic rage and criticism of others, but rather be reasonable and fair in debate, looking for the best in people, weighing things carefully. Let us see behind empty and critical rhetoric, and have courage to listen to God, to discern the wisest course of speech and action, so that bridges of insight and understanding can be built, and a shared way ahead found.

Let us pray:

> Gracious God, you are perfect, holy, good, yet because of Jesus' death on the cross, the one who sacrificed his life for us, you look upon us with grace and mercy. You have reconciled us to yourself in Christ, and now give to us the ministry of reconciliation. Forgive us when we look for the speck in another's eye, whilst there is a log in ours. Give us calm hearts, that we might listen attentively to others, to appreciate their views, even when we differ. May your Holy Spirit inspire a ministry of reconciliation through your people, and in this world, so we might work together for peace and justice, and value and honour one another. In Jesus' name, Amen.

Blog 33: More Bridges – Bridges of Connection

2nd March 2021

All different kinds of connection!

I have been reflecting a lot recently on different ways to connect. In my last blog, I was thinking of the importance of listening and prayerfully making space, but there is so much more to connection.

There are qualities that make deeper connection more possible, openness, love, empathy, compassion. People have such different life experiences, incredibly varied ways of thinking, different priorities, that we need many ways of relating to others.

I was privileged to be a chaplain in a special educational needs school, and I learned so much about different types of communication, whether it was Makaton, dancing or using all the senses. I loved it, and felt at home, as we were all being and learning together.

In this time of lockdown, I worry that so many are becoming isolated, and we are forgetting how to communicate. For many people they have lost their confidence, their ability to relate. And for people who have experienced trauma and sadness, this is intensified.

And so I think we need to build many types of bridges of love and connectivity. I have been reading about 'trauma informed' care often spoken about in education and in medical settings, about helping people to feel safe, to be gentle, to give options, to explain things well, to promote healing and empowerment.

When I hear of this, it seems as natural as breathing. Why haven't we been doing this all the time? And what does it mean for our society, and also in a spiritual dimension. We talk of churches as places of sanctuary, places of safety and healing, but how often is this really the case?

As we start to think a little more about the future, how can we promote healing to a society stressed out and anxious after lockdown, traumatised by experiences of suffering and grief? We need to offer a wide variety of ways to enable people to connect and experience safety and love.

I started to think about many of these themes, because of my late husband's ptsd symptoms and brain injury. And I think how we support individuals, and how we operate as a society, says so much about who we are. We have a choice to pursue divisive and negative rhetoric, or a language that uplifts and offers opportunity for safe self expression.

It says in 1 John 4:19, 'We love because he first loved us.' God revealed the full extent of his love in Jesus, how he challenged corruption, loved the person on the road side, healed the sick. How can we continue that kind of work today, as it has never seemed more important?

Let us pray:

> Gracious God, so many are tired and stressed, lonely and traumatised. Yet you look upon us with tender mercy, and long to pour out your healing balm. Forgive us Lord Jesus, that we are so rigid and narrow in our form of communication, where we often judge others, rather than appreciate their difference. Enlarge our minds and our hearts, through your Holy Spirit, to connect with others with empathy, with creativity, so we can build bridges of acceptance and love with others, Amen.

Blog 34: Spring – the Breath of Life
6th March 2021

Breathing deeply, finding peace

The days are lengthening, there are crocuses on the ground and buds on the trees. Although there are still some rainy dismal days, there is also a feeling of greening, and of spring.

These are still such anxious days, and I am learning more about the importance of breath. We all know breathing is good! But there is so much more to it than this.

In the fresh air, our intuition is to breathe deeply and slowly. We appreciate the air coming into our lungs, that it shows us down, and helps us be more in the moment, at peace and attentive to our environment.

There is so much science to this – that slow, deep breathing reduces anxiety and feelings of panic, that it helps us relax, brings more oxygen to the blood, and releases endorphins. Breathing in should be deep and measured, and breathing out even more slowly. This calms the parasympathetic system and the vagus nerve, and brings a feeling of deep peace. So many practices of Christian meditation reflect the importance of this type of breathing, even from thousands of years before. It is an ancient and healing practice.

Exploring practices that help bring healing to people who are anxious or traumatised, seems so very important in today's age. Whether it is the use of breathing techniques and trauma informed care in schools or medical settings, it seems such a beneficial and holistic tool to offer. In churches also, maybe we need to learn more from ancient Christian meditation practice.

'The breath of the Almighty gives me life' (Job 33:4) and this is not just giving us the capacity for life, but also quality of life and spiritual awareness. The modern worship song 'Sound of our breathing' by Jason Gray, captures something of the rhythm of our breathing, and of God's breath within us.

Let us pray:

> Eternal God, you breathe your life into this world, into every human being – may we notice and cherish this gift. Lord Jesus, when we are stressed or anxious, help us to slow down, and breath deeply, and exhale slowly. Holy Spirit, bring us your healing and calm, shape our lives, and enable us to live more fully for you, Amen.

Blog 35: The Beauty of Nurture
14th March 2021

Mother's Day

see also colour section

Today being mother's day is a very emotional one. I am so fortunate to have my beautiful mum, but have lost my mother-in-law. We owe such a debt to mums and loving patient adults who have helped form us and guided us along our way.

I was so privileged two years ago to attend Bessel van der Kolk's conference on trauma in Boston. It helped me understand so much about trauma, attachment, neurodiversity, body work and different ways of exploring healing for those who are suffering and traumatised. As a lay person, I have so very much to learn.

In the midst of all the technical neurological and psychiatric therapies, a recurring theme was really simple and profound, because what is at the core of it all is the power of love, to create a safe space for people to feel seen, listened to, valued, cherished. Healing can then be explored in different combinations suited to each individual, when some kind of trust can be restored.

It was so exciting, yet so deeply challenging in a world where many feel abandoned, ignored, abused and mistreated. How to be supportive and prayerful, for that broken part within each of us, is so difficult. How can we let God tend to that uncertain, hurting child within?

Listening to stories of the power of good attachment in the earliest years of life, reminded me of the vital nature of good nurture. To support babies and toddlers, to feel safe, and loved, so they can learn and play, can strongly influence children to grow into more contented and peaceful adults. We know this as people, but the scientific data regarding brain formation that confirms this is astounding.

In 2 Timothy chapter 1, we hear of the positive influence his gran Lois, and mum Eunice had on this young boy, in this case passing on their faith to him. It equipped him for his years ahead.

May we know that the choices we make, the attitudes that we have, the love we show, can make such a difference for all around, and especially for babies and children. As we give thanks for mothers' day, may we encourage one another to nurture and love and play with the babies and children in our midst! By doing so, we are building a healthier society.

> Let us pray, Father God, you love us all with a perfect and generous love. Lord Jesus, you delighted in having children around you, and their curiosity and playfulness. Forgive us, as a society, when we let babies and children down, when they feel unsafe and unheard. Holy Spirit, teach us more about how to love and nurture babies and children, and our inner child too, so we can be healthy and whole and at peace, Amen.

Blog 36: Painting and Dancing!

20th March 2021

Free style painting!

Today has been a lovely, dry, spring day, and I decided to paint a wall in the garden. That sounds quite normal, but I had my music on as well, and was listening to the Christian band Hawk Nelson – songs like 'Diamonds', 'Parachute' and 'Never Let You Down'. They are such great songs of faith, I couldn't help but dance. I think I had too much paint on my roller, and I ended up a bit painty, as did the grass, the bush and one or two other things. I think it was quite creative, but rather messy.

Next month will be the third anniversary of my husband's death, and it occurs to me that I still feel guilty for dancing to a song. Some one said it was 'survivor's guilt' that you feel it is not fair to enjoy music when your

loved one can't. It is a way of thinking that is hard to let go.

The grieving process is so lengthy and so complex. You think you are coping with one thing, and then something else starts bothering you, or worse still, something from the past you thought you had worked through, comes back in a new form. It can be so disheartening and exhausting.

Every day, we have to choose once again how to live. We are often sad, or struggling with difficult memories. Yet I believe that part of the healing process, is how to learn to be thankful to God all over again for each day of life. And sometimes that means laughing hysterically, or being still for a long time, or dancing when you are painting! God wants to set us free from grief and sorrow, even just for a few moments. Whatever we are going through, may we all know these moments in life.

We remember God's promise in Isaiah 61:3 'to all who mourn in Zion, God will give a crown of beauty for ashes, a joyous blessing instead of mourning, festive praise instead of despair.'

Let us pray:

> There are so many reasons we may feel sorrowful – illness, the strain of the pandemic, the death of a loved one, and it can feel that the weight of heaviness and darkness will always hang over us. Lord Jesus, you remind us that from the pain and suffering of the cross, came forgiveness and new beginnings. Holy Spirit bring healing to us, so that in moments we might have hope, so we can still dance for joy in your presence, Amen.

Blog 37: What is Life About?

27th March 2021

The big questions!

As a teenager, I remember wondering what life is all about. People talked of leaving school, maybe going to college or university, having a family, retiring, travelling and then there was a pause . . . then we were face to face with our own mortality.

I was searching for answers, and used to wonder if there was a God, and if so what would that God be like, how could I find out. After many questions and discussion and pondering, I came to faith at university, and it was amazing. To look at Jesus's life and ministry, touching those with leprosy, challenging the corrupt, showing tender love to the vulnerable, teaching about forgiveness – that his life revealed the character of God – that blew me away – a God who stands up for truth and justice, yet stoops to pick up the weary – it made perfect sense to me, and still does. The purpose of our lives is to learn to receive Christ's love, and then share it with others. God's love is my anchor and Jesus' teaching and way of living his abundant love poured out for all. And the Holy Spirit revives my soul when I am empty, and strengthens me when I am struggling, and inspires me to imagine a better world, and how to do a tiny part to partner God in this. What a privilege.

'We love because he first loved us.' (1 John 4:19)

Every day, Jesus teaches me more about love. Henri Nouwen's concept of the wounded healer seems central, that somehow through the cross, we find forgiveness and healing, and that through the woundedness of our stories, God can also touch the lives of others.

I so want everyone to know how much they are loved. Whatever your struggles or wounds or difficult memories, Jesus wants to bring healing and wholeness. It is often a process, and can involve many stages and twists and turns, but having Jesus with you makes everything better.

Accompanying Colin, watching his struggles as a veteran, with his head injury and PTSD symptoms and difficulties, meant I learned so much, about prayer, and love and holistic therapies that helped him. He still had such a tough time, but finding prayerful and sympathetic people along the way, made all the difference. And so I am grateful.

For now, I wonder what road God is calling me on, as I want to use what I have learned to support others. I don't have all the answers, but I know that to connect with others seems the greatest privilege in living, to show grace and care, in the same way as God cares so beautifully for us. May we learn to trust him more.

> Dear God, your ways are so much higher than ours, and we can struggle to understand life. We have so many questions. Lord Jesus, on the cross, you show us the true nature of love, to be willing to lay down your life for others. Thank you for all who show such love for others, people in the medical profession, people who are carers, people who serve at home and abroad. Holy Spirit show us our purpose in life, and inspire us to live more closely to our Saviour, and to serve others with the abundant beautiful love that you have shown to us, for surely this is why we are here, Amen.

Blog 38: A Dark Day of Weeping

3rd April 2021

A cascade of tears

Yesterday was Good Friday, always an emotional day. To think that some one could love me enough to give their life for me is so much to take in, never mind that that person is the Son of God.

To read the narratives of the betrayal of Jesus by Judas in the garden, of his trial in front of the high priest, Herod and then Pontius Pilate, and then the crowds shouting 'crucify' is heartbreaking. And then it gets worse, the taunting and mocking of the soldiers, the spitting and jeering and beating, the crown of thorns, Jesus carrying his cross, and then dying on that blood soaked wood.

And the words that Jesus said 'Father, into your hands I commit my spirit,' Luke 23:46, and then breathed his last. I was just so moved by the scene, with his mum Mary, the women, his disciple John all present. Jesus was surrounded by love and prayerful tears, even in the midst of his agony. They watched him commit his spirit to God and breath his last.

And something of the meaning of these words struck home, as I remembered the memory of my late husband breathing his last. The sacredness of that moment, the events leading up to it, the helplessness all came back into focus. And I wept hot tears for Jesus, for Colin, and all with those remembrances of sitting at the bed of a loved one. These moments of eternal significance stay with you for a life time.

It is so hard to finish preparing Good Friday worship, when you cannot see the page in front of you because of your tears. Sometimes the flood gates open, unasked for, as you catch a glimpse of the rawness of grief once again, and that collective grief of the world, sorrowing over loss and pain and sin and violence. It gives a deep sense of the love that motivated Jesus to die for the sins of the world, and to open the way to eternally for all who place their trust in him. And it brings clarity to that sense of the depth of sorrow of those round the cross, accompanying Jesus in that last journey.

Grief is like this, you are thinking that you are getting stronger, and then out of the blue that wave of pain and sorrow overwhelms. It is also a sense of loss that connects with the losses in all humanity, and is so very dark.

The idea that we grieve so much, because we have the privilege of experiencing the richness and fullness of love makes sense. In many ways to feel such pain, is the cost of love, and so it is a privilege. And after tears in the night, eventually comes the comfort of the dawn.

> Gracious Father God, we cannot begin to understand your distress at seeing your precious and beautiful Son so cruelly mistreated at the hands of others. Lord Jesus, even in your darkest moment, you demonstrated love and grace, and trusted your spirit into the hands of your Father. May we know too that sacred moments of life and death are held in your loving and compassionate hands. Even in the midst of our tears, Holy Spirit, help us not to fear, but to trust and find peace, for you are faithful. Thank you Jesus, the lover of our souls, Amen.

Blog 39: Broken, Beloved and Blessed!

10th April 2021

Resurrection in the garden!
(photo taken previous year)

I adore Easter Sunday! I used to get stuck at Good Friday, as I contemplated Jesus on the cross dying for my wrongdoing, saying 'Father, forgive' even in the darkness and pain. The love and amazing grace of our Lord still humbles and astonishes me every day.

However, I have also learned to appreciate the difference resurrection makes, as I think of the women at the tomb, and the words of the angel, 'He is not here, he is risen' (Luke 24:6). The power of these words are breathtaking.

I am going to focus on Mary Magdalene, someone who knew Jesus well, who was described as having 'seven demons' in Luke chapter 8. It is difficult to interpret exactly what that means, but at the very least it means she was troubled or even disturbed. But Jesus healed her, and she became his devoted follower.

So in many ways, Mary went through a time of brokenness, when she was upset, mixed up, distressed. And Jesus helped her find peace. But when she watched her beloved Lord be treated so cruelly, mocked, whipped and beaten, she must have felt so distressed once more, for it seemed that their dream of working for the kingdom of God on earth had died, and their hopes were in smithereens.

In John chapter 20, we have a narrative where the risen Jesus speaks directly to Mary, and calls her tenderly by her name. And she tries to cling to him, but he says it is not the time, for he must ascend to his heavenly Father. The whole encounter between them however, speaks of Mary being beloved to her Lord. She is loved and cherished by him. There is such a depth of beauty in these words, that reminds us that this woman, who was once troubled and seen as an outcast in society, was now accepted and valued.

So Mary was broken, beloved and then blessed. She went to speak to the others, with reverent excitement and enthusiasm saying 'I have seen the Lord'. She has witnessed a miracle, and feels blessed and ready to share what she has seen with the whole world.

This spiritual journey is so relevant to all of us, for we are all struggling or broken without God, but then spending time with Jesus brings healing and an experience of the depth of God's love, that is life changing. And we are blessed so richly, that we are motivated to go out and share our story.

In these days of resurrection, and reflection on the Easter story, may we all find hope and healing and love, so we can travel from brokenness to wholeness, from estrangement to belovedness, from alienation to being blessed. God desires the best for our lives, so may we be open to all he has for us to receive.

May we pray:

> Risen Lord, as you appeared to Mary, please come to each of us, call us by our name, remind us of your healing power and purpose for

our lives. We may have gone though dark days of illness, trauma or grief, but you are still here for us. Speak tenderly to us in our brokenness and tears, and remind us that we are beloved, treasured by you, and that you want to bless us. Holy Spirit, may we be healed and blessed, so we in turn might be a blessing to others. Empower us to do your will, and be a channel of your peace in this world, Amen.

Blog 40: Opening Old Wounds

12th April 2021

The cry for mercy and reconciliation

Watching some of the riots and violent disturbances on the streets of towns and cities in Northern Ireland this week, has been deeply disturbing.

They have brought back memories from the Troubles, when there was much sectarian violent conflict between catholic and protestant factions – knee capping, intimidation, shooting and car bombs.

Commentators and journalists have talked of different causes for this recurrence of violence recently – poverty, provocative words from political leaders on all sides, and the provisions of the Brexit agreement. These are all in danger of reopening old wounds.

My late husband served in Northern Ireland as part of his military career, and his experiences and memories have always reminded me of the price that is paid by all involved in violence – the traumatic memories and the risk of PTSD, as well as the physical injuries. The cost of conflict is so very high and long term, for all involved, and for their families.

The Christian community at Corrymeela, along with many others, have called for people to stand against violence, to show civic courage, and to work towards tolerance, dialogue and reconciliation.

The Corrymeela comment and prayer can be found here. https://m.facebook.com/story.php?story_fbid=10158341299392547& id=76350897546

May we all do our best to work for justice and peace, so that the violence will diminish, and for peaceful but effective ways to be found to support vulnerable and anxious communities. May we pray without ceasing, for peace. Lord, have mercy.

'God was in Christ, reconciling the world to himself, no longer counting people's sins against them. And he gave us this wonderful message of reconciliation.' (2 Corinthians 5:19)

> Gracious God, you long for all people to be reconciled with you in Christ, and also with one another. Forgive us for all the times that we fight and squabble. We pray especially for Northern Ireland, for the violence to stop, and for there to be a will to find a peaceful way forward. Lord Jesus, we know that for many, old memories and hurts are resurfacing, and old wounds being torn open. Forgive us. We give thanks for Corrymeela, and for all who work for peace. Holy Spirit, bring lasting healing to all. In Jesus' name, Amen.

Blog 41: Rays of Light in Times of Heartache

13th April 2021

Sitting with the dying

Today is the 3rd anniversary of my husband's death. Somehow I thought that things would be easier. I have so much to be thankful for, but it is still a time of deep sorrow and difficult memories.

My husband was invalided out of military service because of a blow to the head which resulted in epilepsy. As the years went on, the seizures became more poorly controlled, and this brought degenerative damage to his brain. He was defiantly independent, and tried his best to work through traumatic memories from his service, but as the years went on, he became less able. When he needed 24 hour care, he was admitted to a care home, where they took excellent care of him.

My son, myself and the dog visited regularly, as did other family and friends. However after another 4 years, and a broken hip, he was very weak, and had infection after infection.

And so many times I sat by his bed, with the doctor telling me there was nothing more they could do. All that was left, was to make him comfortable.

So many people sit by the bed of a dying loved one. And we know it is a privilege, time to play beautiful music, to express the things most needing to be said. But is is also exhausting and distressing, watching them gradually become weaker, less able to swallow, the morphine level having to be increased.

At times Colin was restless and agitated, at other times more subdued. At times he knew what you were saying and could respond, with a smile or wave. At times you could give him a little raspberry ripple ice cream – a favourite, and you were rewarded with a wan smile.

It was heartbreaking watching him becoming weaker, shrinking in front of me. On some days, there were rays of light through the window that landed on the bed, bringing him warmth and comfort.

And these rays of light spoke of many things. I was thankful that he was comfortable, and well cared for. I was thankful for family able to visit. I was thankful of the presence of Jesus in the room, ready to take him to be with God, in that moment Colin was ready.

Yet is still hurts – not just Colin's death, but all the years of suffering he experienced, recounting traumatic stories, and having seizures. All the times when he was frustrated and despondent because of his limitations and disabilities. All the years of behavioural issues, of carers and hospital admissions, and the toll it took on his loved ones.

In the last two years, both Colin's parents have died, and that just adds more layers to the trauma and grief.

I pray for all carers looking after a loved one, but especially those sitting at the bedside of a dying relative. I pray for the person not to be in pain, for loving and attentive care, for words of love to be shared, and for a peaceful passing.

And I am thankful for loving family and friends, who prayed for us and supported us, and for moments of humour in the midst of sadness. I am grateful that I have been able to honour Colin's memory by telling his story, and to raise awareness of the plight of veterans. I am glad we could raise money for charity – for the 'Coming Home Centre' in Govan, and for 'Epilepsy Connections' in Glasgow. I am thankful for all these rays of light, and hope and love. But it still hurts . . .

> Eternal Father, you know what it felt like for your precious Son to die on the cross. You know what we humans go through, when we sit with a loved one who is dying. We are anguished and sorrowful. Lord Jesus, thank you that you are there too, with an invitation for people to place their trust in you, and find their eternal home. And that your Holy Spirit enables us to say our goodbyes, and to find peace. Help us as mourn, to honour our loved ones, and then when we are ready, to find our healing, and new direction. May rays of light always fall across our path, Amen.

Blog 42: Healing Memories

17th April 2021

Resting in sunshine

Am so grateful for the glorious weather, and the chance to travel early this morning to Fintry Bay in Millport. It was so very peaceful.

As a result of all the restrictions I haven't been across for over 6 months. Even just getting on the ferry was emotional, the excitement of being on the island after all this time.

Colin's ashes are scattered on the island, so it was a special pilgrimage to go back. And I remembered many events from the past, some difficult, and some connected to the island hospital, which were a bit mixed! Everyone was lovely, and I was so grateful for their care for Colin.

However the beautiful and healing thing, was that every time I turned a corner on the island, good memories came flooding back – Andrew making sand castles on the beach when he was small, all of us playing football on the grass, Colin cheating wildly at crazy golf, walking the dog, getting soaked in torrential rain, having lovely meals together, and just watching the sea in all its majesty, ever changing colours and moods.

Of course, we went cycling as well. Colin had poor balance, but once in the early days, he managed a wee cycle, and the pride on his face that he could cycle faster than his young son! We have a lovely photo of that moment – it was much cherished, because he was so pleased to be able to do something with his son. So often his disability made that difficult. To be able to do this just once, was a treasured memory.

Being on the island today was poignant. At the beginning of the day it was misty, and I couldn't see the hills of Arran. However the mist started to lift as the morning warmed up, and then 'the sleeping warrior' emerged in all its splendour, and things felt peaceful. Colin is at peace.

I am so grateful for memories that remind us of family, friends and pets on the island! Much fun, some adventures even. We were all able to go a couple of trips on the paddle steamer the 'Waverley' and Colin loved this, though I was always worried he would fall off the gang plank! He never did. And so I have a deep sense of thanksgiving for all the joy even in uneven times.

> Creator God, thank you for the gorgeous nature of your creation, the ever changing azure colours, the salt smell of the sea, the call of the seagull. It so tells of your glory. Thank you Lord Jesus for the opportunity to remember, and to notice particularly the fun and the beauty, and to find healing and peace. Holy Spirit, we pray for all who mourn and still struggle, please lead them to memories that can bring assurance and even smiles, and places that bring peace, Amen.

Blog 43: Medication in the Sock Drawer

24th April 2021

There is little logic in the grieving process

There are just so many anniversaries in life. Just when you have worked your way through one, along comes another.

Today is three years to the day since Colin's funeral. Some of the memories are still so vivid, the people who came, the sound of the singing, the positioning of the coffin. My son Andrew and I are so appreciative of all the people who were so supportive and prayerful at this time. It was such an expression of care, at a time of pain and loss.

There is little logic in it. As the grieving person, you begin to realise that you are not only missing the person, but also your old way of life together. You also begin to realise that habits you adopted, especially to support a loved one who was unwell or disabled, are no longer appropriate.

An example of this, was that one of the conditions my late husband had was epilepsy. This meant that anytime we went anywhere, the first thing we did was check we had his medication with us. If we were going abroad, I would have it in my hand luggage as well as the cargo hold, just in case. It is drilled into my head to take Colin's medication everywhere I go.

So this is not working for me now! I need to retrain my brain not to think of this. But it is very hard. And so my confession today is that I have kept some epilepsy medication in my sock drawer, just in case. Just in case of what, I don't know, but it it just one step too far to dispose of it. In my head I know this is ridiculous, but my heart just doesn't want to let go.

So when people say they are still struggling with grief, even three years on, please be kind. The multilayered significance of the loss of of the person, their life, their life together, and a way of living, is so hard to articulate. There are so many decisions and accommodations that you make in life, that then have to be relearned. It is a slow, laborious process of reformation, but God strengthens us and gently leads us forward, for he shows mercy to the sorrowful.

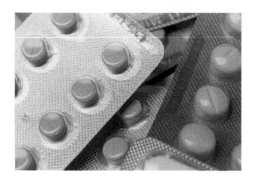

'God heals the broken hearted, and binds up their wounds.' (Psalm 147:3)

Gracious and eternal God, we give thanks that You understand our hurts and sadnesses and convoluted thinking. Lord Jesus, thank you that you are gentle with those who are sorrowful, and heavy in heart. Holy Spirit, help us to become unstuck from repeating old ways that were so important in the past. Lead us from grief and old patterns of thinking and being, so we can find healing and freedom to be our true selves. Amen.

Blog 44: The Power of Telling our Story

11th May 2021

Learning to speak

In recent weeks, I have been mulling over the power of telling your story. It is perhaps a bit of a cliche, but there is something that is cathartic about trying to put something you experienced into words. It helps you to reinterpret the significance of what happened, and to understand it in a different way. You often notice something that you hadn't seen before.

It might look a bit selfish to be focused on telling your story. Yet I think the purpose is a deeper understanding of our humanity, and the connection that exists between us all. And you hope this might help another human being. Some one said, 'The courage it takes to tell your story might be the very thing some one needs to open their heart to hope.'

This spring was three years after Colin's death. I thought enough time has passed to make things more bearable, and I was taken aback by the pain all over again. This is not just about his death, but also about the trauma and behaviours around epilepsy and brain injury. So many difficult memories.

I am not saying this because I am looking for sympathy. Rather I am just saying this because that's where I am at. The processes of grief don't follow a neat path, but are an emotional storm that is unbridled and turbulent.

So I write this to help others who are grieving. So often people say 'you should be over this by now' but it really doesn't work like that. All we can do is find the courage to say where we are at.

I started to tell my husband Colin's story to honour his memory, but in doing this, I told our story. I had to decide which bits to leave out, or to focus on, so there is always an interpretative context. Doing this, and writing *Love Song for a Wounded Warrior* has changed me, it has helped me look into a time of suffering and pain, and to try to speak to challenge people about the suffering of veterans and their families. It has helped me notice things about myself, which have been hard to face, but which ultimately will be therapeutic.

In her book *The Gifts of Imperfection* Brene Brown said, 'Owning our story and loving ourselves through the process is the bravest thing we will ever do.' I can understand that because I feel vulnerable and sad, and for many years I kept it all to myself. To speak of some of what happened has been tough, but also feels like a calling.

To anyone who is reading this, thank you. I think of Rick Warren's words, 'Other people are going to find healing in your wounds. Your greatest life messages and your most effective ministry will come out of your deepest hurts.' That is my prayer.

In the midst of all this, my Christian faith has been my strength. In psalm 45, the NLT translation it says: 'Beautiful words stir my heart. I will recite a lovely poem about my King, for my tongue is like then pen of a skillful poet'. I am not a skillful poet, but I do feel called to tell this story, to write, to connect, to seek to tell others of the wonders of God's love, even in the darkest of moments, and to encourage and bring hope.

> Gracious God, your story is told in your beautiful book, the Bible being full of your grace and love towards a broken and fragile humanity. Lord Jesus, things happen in life that are so difficult, beyond the power of words to tell. Yet I thank you that you understand. Bring healing to all those who suffer and are in pain. Holy Spirit, give us the courage to tell our individual stories, however messy, and somehow may they bless others. And as we speak, may we also find fresh insights, which enable us to grow stronger and find deeper peace, Amen.

Blog 45: The Shenanigans of Seagulls

15th May 2021

It looks harmless, but . . .

Yesterday I travelled north (before the new covid restrictions were announced) and was walking along the streets in the town in which I had newly arrived. All was going well till splat, and a present arrived from a passing seagull. So there I was, in the middle of the street, trying to remove bird splatter from my hair with dollops of hand sanitiser. Not the best moment in my day. I got some very strange looks.

It reminded me that I have often found that in times of stress, trauma or bereavement, other things often go wrong. It could be a little thing, like forgetting something, or getting your jumper sleeve caught in the handle of a door you were endeavouring to go through. The week after my husband's funeral, I took my son to the cinema, in the forlorn hope of distracting ourselves for a moment, and I managed to break a bone in my foot. In the cinema! How is that even possible?

I think though if you are a long term carer, or have been bereaved, so much of your brain is coming to terms with what happened, another part becomes less active, and you can become accident prone. The stress of everything on your body, seems to show itself in clumsiness, illness and even pantomime situations where ridiculous things happen. A grief reaction I hadn't been aware of, is to laugh hysterically at something. I think it was the alternative to crying, but it looked a bit strange. I still do this!

I just want to encourage anyone who is going through difficult days, when things seem to go wrong around you. It can be so frustrating. It doesn't last forever, or hopefully at least not in such an intense way!

In the midst of all the antics that happen to us, and around us, I remember the verse from Psalm 3: 'You, O Lord, are a shield around me, my glory, the lifter of my head.'

When we feel besieged by adversity, God shields us with his love. When we are down, God lifts up our head, and gives us hope. What a great God we have.

> Creator God, we thank you for all the creatures in this world, even seagulls! We know that when we feel sad or under strain, it can seem that everything is going wrong. Lord Jesus, may we know your understanding presence with us, and find strength, and be able to find a way forward. Holy Spirit, console us when we are discouraged, help us to be patient, and to keep trusting, Amen.

Blog 46: After the Rain . . .

22nd May 2021

I was fortunate enough to be away for a few days up north. I so appreciated the change from the normal frantic pace of life, to a time of space and light and rest. I was so blessed. The weather was often amazing, but there was a particular day when you could see the black clouds gathering up ahead. There was nothing I could do, but wait for the inevitable rain. The deluge was heavy and torrential and the puddles deep.

However, after the rain, it was magical. There is a softness in the light, and the whole of creation seems to be coated with a reflective shimmer, that adds brilliance to all things. It was magnificent.

Often we question why there is so much suffering in the world, so much heartache and pain. There are no easy answers to these profound wrestlings about meaning and purpose.

Yet often on our journey, we find that after the rain and the sorrow, we develop a patience and a softness to us, that we have learned in the midst of trauma and sadness. We learn what is important, and what really doesn't matter at all.

The temptation when skies are dark, is to become overwhelmed, to doubt, to become full of self pity or resentment. Why has God allowed this to happen, we shout.

Yet, even in the darkest and coldest experiences, we discover the tender presence of Jesus alongside us, we find a flicker of light, an act of kindness that brings comfort and a deep sense of connection. And these moments transform all things, and help us trust that God is still good.

I was thinking of the verse from Leviticus 26:4: 'I will send you rain in season, and the ground will yield its crops, and the trees their fruit.' Even the rain has a purpose, and can bring new life and growth.

> Creator God, you have created a beautiful world of light and shadow, rain and sunshine, heat and cold. Every experience can have significance and purpose, and we learn from each one. Lord Jesus, you teach us that after the most terrifying storm, can come peace, and that after rain can come a deep calm and serenity. Whatever adversity we have faced, or are facing, may your Holy Spirit help us to find a deeper insight and new perspective, which brings us wisdom which we can share with others, and draws us closer to you, Amen.

Blog 47 After Bereavement, Who are We?

29th May 2021

Intertwined reflections

I used to think that once you lost some one you loved, that you were sad for a while, and then felt better. However often, grieving is such a complex process, and can be confusing and circular in form. You often seem to go round in a circle, rather than making tangible progress.

One of the things I struggle with, is about identity. Often in a marriage, you get to know the other person so well, you almost become one. And when the two people are no longer together, you can't remember who you were beforehand. Another dimension can be if you are a carer, as your energy in in supporting your loved one, and your motivation and focus is their wellbeing. When that person is gone, you miss them profoundly.

But you also can realise that you have then lost your self too. The simplest decisions seem too hard.

Part of the grieving process then, is allowing your wounds to heal, and then seeking space to find out what is left in who you are. It can be hard to remember, and the old 'you' is gone anyway. So I pray for God to refashion me into whoever I am meant to be now, a bizarre mix of genetics, memories, learning and likes and dislikes, limitations and scars.

We can work hard on trying to work out our new priorities, praying for inspiration, seeking wise counsel. Yet I think perhaps the best thing, is to pray for God to shape our lives, to remind us that he still has a purpose for us. In Isaiah, the prophet writes 'Yet you, Lord, are our Father. We are the clay, you are the potter; we are all the work of your hand.' (Isaiah 64:8)

At times that can be what we feel like – a clump of heavy mishapen clay. Yet God is not finished with us yet, and can use even our cracks and blemishes, to make something beautiful. Though his Spirit, may we each find our God given identity as his beloved child, and have courage to live in this truth, and to find our way forward.

> Gracious God, you tell us in your word, that we are made in your image, and that we are fearfully and wonderfully made. Help us remember this when have many questions, and we feel lost and disorientated. Lord Jesus bring healing to us, and in time help us rediscover our true self. In this season of Pentecost, may your Holy Spirit bring life to dry bones, so that we might live again. In Jesus' name, Amen.

Blog 48: Support and Inspiration on the Journey

31st May 2021

Beauty and connection bring healing

It is a beautiful sunny day, a day to reflect on what I am learning. Even with my lack of understanding and weakness, I want to share this to seek to be a blessing to others.

It is over three years since my husband died. Foolishly, at this point, I thought this was rock bottom. I was a mixture of emotions – numb, exhausted, traumatised, desolate. What I learned subsequently, was that I had buried so much, that I was not even aware it was there. A mixture of grief, vicarious trauma and painful memories. As Colin was a veteran, he suffered in his life, and that impacted not just him, but also his family. Gradually it has all surfaced, and I am so grateful to those who have so patiently supported me on this journey of complex grief.

So what has helped? Beauty on the journey, the amazing restorative power of nature, especially water, the mischievous presence of my dogs, listening for hours to Christian praise music, retreats, the prayerful support of friends, the love of family. I am so blessed.

Another dimension which is crucial in my journey, is the work of Bessel van der Kolk and Bruce Perry. They have revolutionised my understanding of trauma, its impact on the body as well as the soul, enabling holistic ways of healing.

In recent weeks I have been reading a book *What Happened to You?* describing a series of conversations between Bruce Perry and Oprah Winfrey on trauma, resilience and healing. I would really recommend this book, as a great introduction to this topic. It gives lots of information about the spectrum of trauma, and how to find healing. A whole spectrum of neuro-sequential tools are offered, with the concept of regulate, relate, reason (page 279).

In the midst of the information about different forms of therapy, Bruce Perry talks a lot about the importance of healing communities, including dance, music, sports. And he says that even better than a great therapist (although that is highly recommended), is 'having access to family, community and culture . . .with cognitive, relational based and sensory elements.'[10] Connectedness is one of the greatest elements of healing, being seen and been heard.

People who have taken the time to hear me, have been so significant on my journey. And I pray everyone who feels marginalised, neglected or alone, will find a safe place to tell their story, and can find a community to connect with, where they will be valued. And it gives me a vision of what I think church should ideally be like, a place where God welcomes every individual, and brings healing to those who feel broken. I feel called to seek to develop this, but I am such an early stage.

I just want to thank you for reading, and if you have any ideas or inspiration, please do share them. I would love for there to be more places of safety and healing for people who are in difficult or dark places. As a community, may we do what we can.

> Gracious God, your presence is always a place where we can find refuge, safety, love and acceptance – thank you. Lord Jesus, you experienced so much trauma and suffering in your life, so much injustice. We weep at the way you were treated in this world. Yet Lord, out of the darkest, painful experiences in our lives, help us to find a wisdom that might help others. So many suffer and are fearful and restless. May your Holy Spirit encourage us to find our healing path, and as we grow stronger, to share what we have learned to offer this to others, Amen.

---

10 Bruce Perry, *What Happened to You?* Pan Macmillan, 230.

Blog 49: Seizures and Grace

6th June 2021

Person in distress

My late husband Colin had epilepsy. It sounds like such a little word, but it had such major consequences. He was unfortunate, in that his epilepsy was intractable, and so he would have 4-6 tonic clonic seizures a month, always when he was asleep.

A seizure would start with a loud guttural shout, the change of colour of skin and shaking of limbs, and then his body becoming more limp, and the gradual restoration of a more rhythmic natural breathing occurred. It could appear pretty scary. Colin was again unfortunate, in that he had long post-ictal periods, so his brain function would not be fully restored for days.

My heart goes out to all who live with this disability. I know that many people have epilepsy that is well controlled by medication, and they have a good quality of life. However for those whose epilepsy is more difficult to manage, my prayers are especially with you, your family and friends.

I guess this is where the grace comes in. It seems like grace, when people around you are understanding. Grace when people call an ambulance when some one has a seizure on the street. Grace when people choose not to walk by on the other side of the road.

We were fortunate too, to have good support from various organisations, including 'Epilepsy Connections'. This organisation provided great practical support, as well as a brilliant befriender. From another similar organisation, we found another support worker, who understood the nuances of how seizures can affect you, and was a brilliant help to Colin, even in demanding and unusual situations. So much grace.

Sadly I know from much personal experience how difficult it can be to support some one living with epilepsy. However it is certainly never dull, and teaches you much about love! I hope that as a society, we might be better informed about seizures, and more open to learning, and being supportive, and I am grateful for all who work in this difficult area of medicine and social care.

In the bible, Jesus often met people having seizures, and was able to heal them, as in Matthew 4:24. My prayer is that there would be many opportunities for healing for people with this condition.

> Gracious God, you want all people to be well, to be loved, to be at peace. Yet in our world we see such suffering and illness, including epilepsy, cancer and other diseases and conditions. Lord Jesus bring healing, through your love and power, through medicine, and through wise individuals, willing to go the extra mile. Holy Spirit, when people are ill and distressed, by your grace, may there always be some one there to care, to helpfully intervene and to bless, for in that way God's kingdom comes, Amen.

Blog 50: Comfort and Deep Sorrow

13th June 2021

Attempting not to be overwhelmed

I am grateful that I live in a country where I have been able to have my two vaccinations against covid19. I know they should help prevent the virus affecting me severely in the future, and that is a great blessing.

However, I am also cognisant of the many millions of people in other lands, who have no access to effective medical care, never mind a vaccination programme. And it means I live in a state of comfort, but also great sorrow. Although sometimes I cannot bear to watch the news, I can still see the pictures in my heart of people struggling to get medical help for their loved ones, in hospitals that are overwhelmed. Their tears and cries of lament and despair are everywhere.

This is perhaps an empathetic response. It is the same with people diagnosed with cancer or other medical condition, and that feeling of shock and bewilderment. Or being aware of the cries of wounding and terror on battlefields, echoing throughout the years. Glencoe, however hauntingly beautiful, is a place where you are conscious of the massacre that took place there.

We have to self care, to focus on what is true, noble, right, pure, lovely, admirable, excellent and praiseworthy, as it says in Philippians 4:8, but we cannot forget the cries of those living on the margins, the sick, the lonely, the traumatised, the impoverished. These are people with names and stories, and they are hurting.

Feeling it is part of our humanity. How we respond us the next step? We might pray, for particular friends, groups of people or countries in need. We might choose to give to a charity that works there, or to encourage a friend who works on the front line. In some circumstances we might be called to raise awareness, or even to go there ourselves.

I love Christianity, as it is not remotely airbrushed. The Bible shows human nature for all it us, at times brutal and nasty, at other times courageous and self sacrificial, the best and worst of humanity nature. And on the cross, Jesus saw the worst of humanity the cruelty and callousness with which he was treated, and sins of the world. And yet he said ' Father, forgive them for they know not what they are doing.' (Luke 23:34) And he showed that love can overcome even the most awful malevolence.

We remember some of the words of Desmond Tutu: '**Goodness is stronger than evil, love is stronger than hate, light is stronger than darkness**'.

May these words minister to our souls.

> Gracious and everlasting God, sometimes it can all seem too much, the cries of the wounded and neglected and damaged. We are in danger of being consumed by sorrow. Yet Lord Jesus, by your life and example, you call us to transform that pain, into a strength to do what we can, to pray and love and act, to love mercy and to act justly. Holy Spirit, forgive us when it is too much, and we just sit in a corner and howl. Please lift us up, and inspire us to get involved, and to be on the side of the angels, Amen.

Blog 51: On the Alert – a Carer's Relationship with their Phone!

19th June 2021

When we have a loved one who is vulnerable or unwell, the sound of your phone becomes crucial. Whatever you are doing, your phone is always nearby, and you are on edge listening for it to ring. Whether it is a child struggling at school, a loved one in a care home, or a relative in hospital, your phone is that vital conduit of the latest information, and as such becomes central in your life.

When the phone goes off, my first instinct was to worry, what has happened, what can be done, what decision needs to be made. It is like the rest of the world is on hold in that moment, as you digest this latest twist in their care, and what it might mean. Time slows down, and is almost still.

I love when the person on the other end of the phone understands that, and starts their sentence, 'Now I don't want you to worry, but . . .' It just seems so humane, and gives you time to adjust to what was coming next.

With my late husband, phone calls could mean he had a seizure, an infection, or in some instances that he needed to go to hospital. Sometimes I needed to go straight away, morning, noon or night, and it became the norm for me to be ready to do so. But that meant I became on high alert every time I heard the sound of the phone, as I never knew what to expect.

I don't know if my relationship with my phone will ever be normalised. I believe that Colin is now safe with Jesus, so I am not going to get emergency calls about him in the middle of the night. However, when the phone goes . . .

And so in every circumstance, I need to trust in God, and to seek to be calm. In Psalm 28 verse 7 it says, 'The Lord is my strength and my shield. I trust him with all my heart.' As we all learn to trust God more, may we panic less, even when the phone goes!

A prayer:

> Gracious God, we thank you for all who care for others, and do so with love and grace. We thank you for people on phones, who quickly communicate vital information. Lord Jesus, you encircle us with your love, you communicate your care for all who are struggling. May we learn to hear the phone ring without being fearful or catastrophising. May your Holy Spirit guide us, and bring healing, and peace. Amen.

Blog 52: The Book Launch June 2020

22nd June 2021

This week, it will be a year since the publication of *Love Song for a Wounded Warrior* a book aimed at telling the story of the late Colin Gardner, to publish his poetry and writings of his time in the military, and to share something of his experiences as a civilian coping with disability and trauma. The book was published in June 2020, to honour his wish that his story be published for the benefit of others.

I am so thankful to everyone who has shared this journey with us, with grace, patience and prayer. I am so thankful for those who have listened and shared insights. I am so thankful for people who have become more aware of the plight of veterans, who often just can't come to terms with what they have been through, and who struggle profoundly.

Love Song for a Wounded Warrior is available by contacting me directly, or through Amazon. It costs £10, and all the proceeds are split between the 'Coming Home Centre' in Govan, and 'Epilepsy Connections'. So far, over £3,200 has been raised, so thank you again. There is purpose in raising money for these two excellent charities, so others might be supported.

One of the outcomes of this process that I did not understand when I set out, was the privilege of getting to know a new online community interested in this theme. It has been a joy to hear your stories and we all seek to support each other. It feels like a healing community, gathered under this umbrella.

I found it very difficult to share our story – it was too intensely private and personal. A song that really helped me was Mandisa's *Born for This* based on the story of Esther. The idea is that there is there are times you feel compelled to speak, even if you are not invited, you don't have the floor, but you feel you need to stand apart from the crowd, and find courage to speak.

This story is a tough read. Colin's experiences were harrowing, and for us as a family trying to help him find the support to find peace, it was messy, frustrating and often bewildering. In the midst of it, our Christian faith gave us strength, and there were many poignant and humerous moments!

I am really humbled by people's responses, and would encourage all of us to have the courage to speak, even when we feel hesitant or if feels painful. Much prayerful discernment is needed, and talking it through with the people closest to us, and listening to God. Sometimes however, we just can't remain silent . . .

Over this anniversary week, I hope to blog a few times about some of the themes of the book, and why I want to raise awareness. As a Christian too, I want people to have freedom to be able to express the messiness, heartbreak and trauma of life. Life is often tough, and we need to be real. Hopefully this encourages others to realise that they are not alone.

I am inspired by Psalm 45:1 – this is the New Living Translation: 'Beautiful words stir my heart; I will recite a lovely poem about the King, for my tongue is like the pen of a skilful poet.'

I am not a skilful poet, but I do want to honour God, by telling our story, and the difference that Jesus has made in our lives, so that it might encourage others in difficult and painful places.

> Gracious Father, you are our hiding place in life's storms, and you keep us safe. Lord Jesus, you understand the ugliness and sadness of our stories, and you are with us, holding us in your love, forgiving our doubts and rebellion, and reminding us of your presence, even in the darkest places, when we feel alone and afraid. May your Holy Spirit always guide us, to reveal when we should be silent, and when we should speak, and may all our stories be a blessing and encouragement to others, Amen.

Blog 53: Transforming Wounds into Scars

23rd June 2021

Wounds of trauma

There is a quotation from the American military leader Douglas MacArthur: 'The soldier, above all other people, prays for peace, for he must suffer and bear the deepest wounds and scars of battle.'

This week, I witnessed the aftermath of a road traffic accident, where a car hit a cyclist. The cyclist, a young man had a gash to his head, and was bruised and on a state of shock, and taken off in an ambulance.

Seeing his injuries, got me in touch with that feeling of what being wounded can feel like, the initial surprise, feeling faint, the pain, the blood. It is such a debilitating thing, where you feel helpless and vulnerable.

For many people, including veterans, our wounds are not just physical but also emotional and psychological. Past traumas can stop you functioning, as powerful memories replay in your mind, paralysing you, and stopping you function. Triggers, which bring buried memories back, can cause reactions which look random, but which are part of people's coping strategies, and these strategies then often become part of the problem.

How can these wounds be healed? If it is a bodily injury, a wound needs to stop bleeding, for it to be cleaned out, and then for healing to take place. Wounds can be prone to infection, so sometimes they need to be cleaned out again, for ointment or antibiotics to be used. The healing can be itchy and uncomfortable, but eventually a scar is formed, at first looking angry and raw, but eventually fading.

For emotional and traumatic wounds, there is a similar process. There are practitioners in traumatic therapies, that can help people acknowledge the terror and the pain, and start the journey of cleansing, forgiveness and healing. The book *The Body Keeps the Score* by Bessel van der Kolk demonstrates the range of possible neurological and community based programmes that can help.

In parallel to this, as a Christian, the balm of Gilead comes to mind. In Isaiah 1:6, the prophet describes a broken nation: 'From the sole of your foot to the top of your head, there is no soundness, only wounds and bruises and open sores, not cleansed or bandaged or soothed with oil.' In a similar situation in Jeremiah 8:22 the prophet asks 'is there no balm in Gilead?' This balm was an aromatic and antiseptic medicine, to bring healing. The balm is often interpreted as the soothing and restorative love and presence of Jesus himself.

To transform wounds to scars, is a surprisingly raw and long process. It can involve prayer, the transformative healing power of Jesus Christ, and an understanding and loving community around you. It can involve wise and sensitive trauma therapies which allow the wound to be cleansed, and for deeper and lasting healing to take place. The scars will always remain, and they are not something to be ashamed of, but they are part of our story.

Let us pray:

> Gracious God, as a world we are so broken, and we hurt and are in pain – so much violence and cruelty. Lord Jesus Christ, thank you that you are the wounded healer, and that you come alongside us, and remind us of the scars you bear. May your Holy Spirit guide us to individuals and communities that are supportive and wise. May despair and darkness never overwhelm us, for there is always forgiveness and love and hope. May the oil of Gilead flow, and bring healing to all haunted by traumatic pasts, to transform open wounds into healthy scars. May we all be channels of your grace and peace to others, Amen.

Blog 54: Legacy of Love

24th June 2021

In memory of Colin

Today is the actual anniversary day of the booklaunch of *Love Song for a Wounded Warrior*. I am so grateful for all who have been so supportive, prayerful and understanding to our story. That has made such a difference.

I started writing Colin's story because I was journalling. I have kept a prayer journal for many years. When Colin became too unwell to complete his writings, I wanted to use my writings to give context to his words, to try to explain that they were fragments of his experiences, because over time to lost the capacity to relate his memories. I hope to eventually feel a sense of completion to have honoured his wishes in this way. Thank you to all of you for helping me do this.

One of the things I learned about Colin's complex military traumas was that he felt better when he told his story, was heard and understood. He felt alive telling stories about his experiences, whether it was a critical incident or a car bomb. And so there is something so powerful about sharing something of your interior life, and being heard, even if just by one person.

For me, Colin has left a legacy of love. He showed me what courage looked like, humour in the face of distress, defiance against the odds, faith in no man's land, in a bleak and desolate territory of nothingness.

So, now I have to ask God to continue my healing, and remind me of my purpose to let these experiences enable me to in turn support others. I want to use my legacy learnings for good in the world. God is guiding me through this process, and I am so grateful. One of my learnings is that I really enjoy writing, and I want to continue this, at least for this season. I think I want to write some more contemplative pieces also, so there might be more variety in what I offer.

In the *Four Quartets* T.S. Eliot wrote, 'In my end is my beginning'. The circularity of life cycles is striking, and I pray that for all of us, in the midst of grief and painful endings, new buds and new life will emerge.

I often go back to the words of Jesus: 'I tell you the truth, unless a grain of wheat falls to the ground and dies, it remains a single seed. But if it dies, it produces many seeds.' (John 12:24)

This helps me make sense of life, for sometimes dreams, familiar ways of thinking, even people have to die. But in the mystery of all things, there gradually emerges new life and possibilities.

For anyone struggling with trauma, fear and grief, I desire healing and new possibilities for you. It is a difficult road, but our Saviour walks with us, and we explore the legacy of his love forever.

> Gracious God, you know all things, you love us, and redeem our life from the pit, and crown us with love and compassion. When we are deep in that dark pit however, we grumble and complain and cry out to you, for we feel scared and alone. And through the cross, Lord Jesus, you offer us cleansing, forgiveness, acceptance and renewal of spirit. You embrace us with the blanket of your love, and keep us safe. May we humbly receive your grace. Give us courage to tell our story, and to find our healing. May your Holy Spirit help us honour legacies of love, and use our learnings and insights to be an encouragement and blessing to others, Amen.

Blog 55: The Frustration of Invisible Disabilities

3rd July 2021

Hidden dangers?

Disabilities, things we struggle to do, for whatever reason, can be so frustrating. They can be seen or unseen – but still hugely significant to the individual involved. My late husband for example, had a problem with proprioception – estimating depth. This sounds like a small thing, but it meant he had issues doing something as simple as pouring tea, because he would overfill it, and the burning liquid would go everywhere. It also affected his gait, as he couldn't tell when his foot would hit the ground, so he

would be uncertain of each footstep, and more likely to fall.

I have been listening to people with disabilities recently, and some of the indignities endured. We think we are a modern inclusive society, but if you have ever used a wheelchair you discover that this is not true. A floor is uneven, a pavement kerb is too high, and even a disability friendly toilet, doesn't seem to mean you can turn round in a wheelchair. There are so many obstacles to keeping your dignity. The only consolation, is that there are also many kind people who are ready to help out and go the extra mile.

For disabilities not able to be seen, the issues are just as distressing. Whether it is a neurological condition or a lung problem, or any one of many health conditions, people are often not noticing or dismissive. We live in a society that is often so judgmental. A person I knew with

Parkinsons for example, was often treated as if they were drunk, and given no help if in difficulty.

People shouldn't have to be expected to explain themselves in order to be treated with respect. There are perhaps some practical possibilities of dealing with specific situations. One person talked of having to go out of a cafe to the toilet for example, and they come back and their table with their fresh coffee and not eaten food is cleared. Can we have a nationally recognised card, to leave, to secure a place in a queue or at a table? We need better training too, with people perhaps having to spend a day in a wheelchair to see just what it is like.

In general, the deeper question is how to change people's awareness and attitudes, to become a kinder, more compassionate society. Then if we see some one struggle, instead of ignoring them, we ask how we might be supportive. It might be we can't do anything, but the knowledge of a sympathetic person can go a long way.

In Colossians 3:12b it says: 'You must clothe yourselves with tenderhearted mercy, kindness, humility, gentleness and patience.'

This is the best way to live, to choose every morning to be kind and compassionate, to show the same mercy and patience as Christ has shown to us.

> Gracious God, forgive us that we often react to people who seem different with fear or prejudice. We are too quick to judge someone who takes their time, or is boisterous. Lord Jesus forgive our lack of curiosity and patience. Teach us how to love, with the mercy and forgiveness you show us. May your Holy Spirit give us insight, and to teach us how to accept and value others, as beautifully as you do us, Amen.

Blog 56: God Desires Restoration for our Souls

7th July 2021

Photo of Luskentyre beach, Outer Hebrides – see colour section

After dark times of trauma, grief and pandemic stresses and worries, we might all be forgiven if our mood is a little uneven. It is going to take a long time, maybe even generations for there to be healing or recovery for those who have experienced some of the bleak and tragic consequences of the impact of coronovirus.

When we feel overwhelmed or sad, many things help, the power of prayer, a listening ear, a promise kept, a thoughtful message, the paw proffered by a pet. God uses so many ways to lift up our souls, and to remind us we are loved.

One of the things I am learning to appreciate more and more is the stunning nature of Scottish countryside, especially the western islands. There are so many epic landscapes, towering cliffs, colourful machairs, dramatic coastlines, exquisite beaches, and an amazing variety of birds and creatures. Even in the drizzle, these have the power to speak to our soul of big emotions, of wilderness and tragedy and solace and inspiration. The stories from each community visited are so moving.

I am reading from the Passion translation of the bible just now, and in Psalm 148 verse 1 it says:

> Hallelujah! Praise the Lord. Let the skies be filled with praise, and the highest heavens with shouts of glory.

Just connecting with Creation, can remind us of the glory and majesty of God, so that just for a while, our hurts and wounds can seem smaller. Just being able to be still enough to give thanks and to worship, reorientates us, and can bring hope and restoration to our souls. Whether it is the shrill call of a bird, changing light through the clouds, or the rhythm of the waves – may we be lost in wonder, awe and praise. If we have opportunity in this summer period, may we intentionally spend time in some of our glorious landscapes, and to find God, and in him, refreshment and hope.

> Gracious God, at times our hearts are bruised by worry and grief – our cares are heavy, and often beyond words. Please speak to us that word in season that we need to hear. Creator of all, as we experience the grandeur of your creation, may tears of appreciation run down our faces, as we bow down before you in worship and thanksgiving. Lord Jesus, help us to experience your love in new ways, and find a broader perspective on our troubles. Holy Spirit, in your creation, may we find restoration for our souls, and your healing grace and peace, Amen.

Blog 57: Landscape of Lament

10th July 2021

A cleit and dwelling places at St Kilda

I had the privilege of visiting St Kilda this week. It is a group of islands over 40 miles from Uist off the west coast of Scotland, where for thousands of years, people lived in a very harsh enviroment. The group of islands and stacs are stunningly beautiful, with incredible rock formations, a vast and varied colony of birds, including puffins, and the physical remains of a community, who chose to leave in 1930, when the community was no longer viable. When we visited, the cloud was often very low, and it gave it all a very atmospheric and mysterious air.

Walking around the village, you can see the remains of blackhouses (traditional stone cottages from the 1830s), almost 1,300 cleits (stone larders), dykes, the church, the factor's house, graveyard etc. There are sheep everywhere, and you can imagine a little of trying to work the land, looking after the sheep, and capturing birds for harvesting.

Traditionally in Scottish literature, the relationship between humanity and the land is depicted as harsh. Think of the writer George Douglas Brown, depicting rural life as cruel and desolate in *The House with the Green Shutters*. Or we might look at Lewis Classic Gibbon's *A Scots Quair*, and the changes that war brought to the farming community. People often work hard in all weathers, only for the crops to fail, or financial ruin to strike.

We sometimes have an ideal concept of farming life, but listening to the stories of the people on St Kilda soon dispels this. They were out in the fields in all weathers, and in the evenings spinning and crafting wool, distilling oil for export from birds, making skins into shoes etc, and often living with their animals. Life is depicted as relentless, and yet the people persevered, through illness and little medical support, and terrible storms, when the community were completely cut off. You can't help but admire their stoicism. And when you visit, you almost hear the song of lament in the air, for the loss of so many lives over generations.

Today, we perhaps face different types of adversities and obstacles, sometimes more subtle ones, but they are there – poor health, the loss of work opportunities, the impact of the pandemic, climate change, injustice in our society. We have to try to navigate these, whilst keeping our self respect, and a constructive sense of purpose.

Christians are not exempt from seasons of frustration and hardship. Everyone has to work through difficult stuff. Yet God always encourages people to keep going, and to have hope, even when things are tough.

In Galatians 6:9 it says: 'Let us not grow weary of doing good, for in due season, we will reap if we do not give up.'

> Creator God, you have made this beautiful world, yet we live in a state of rebellion and disharmony, and it is hard work to care for nature, and to make a living. We give thanks for those who persevere in what seem like impossible circumstances. Sometimes we lament for the pain people experience just trying to put food on the table, and we think of story of the people in St Kilda in the past, and many other places today. Lord Jesus, help us all to work together for a just and fairer world. And when it all seems too much, Holy Spirit give us courage to persevere, and hope that things can get better, Amen.

Blog 58: Sunset Reflections

11th July 2021

Sunset in Lewis

Sometimes I forget to slow down. I try to do too many things, I am always trying to catch up.

So one evening this week, I decided just to sit and watch the sun go down. It couldn't be hurried, so I just sat and waited and reflected. It was a gorgeous still evening, with a soft light falling over the fields. Sometimes in the past, Colin and I would watch the sunset, and it was a time of connection and wonder.

The sunset was a time of aching beauty. It was breathtakingly gorgeous, but was also about change and letting go.

In the last 18 months, there has been so much heartache, pain and loss, through the pandemic and all the implications for so many lives. Times of questioning, isolation, depression, sadness. And in the midst of this, also stories of courage, humour and self sacrifice, as people sought to support others. Key workers, neighbours and others going the extra mile.

Gazing at the setting sun, was a moment that Wordsworth might have called a 'spot in time' – a glimpse into eternity, a realisation of just how fragile life is, how easily it can slip away. And a deep appreciation for each day that we are given.

In Psalm 90, the psalmist says, 'Teach us to number our days , that we might gain a wisdom of the heart'.

There is something profound in this, that we need to treasure each new day we have, for none of us knows how long we have. Sometimes the days fly by, and we wonder what we have achieved. In the midst of all things, may we take time to slow down, to ponder and to pray. If this was our last day on earth, what would we do? What is important to us? What is holding us back?

I am coming to the end of my break in the Outer Hebrides. It has been a time of stunning beauty, outstanding journeys, amazing wildlife, and of healing and space. I have loved this time. And watching that sunset, was a time of communion with God, of recalling the past, coming to terms with the present, and seeking purpose for the days to come. Whatever our situation, may God speak to each one of us that word of encouragement we need to hear, as we continue onward.

> Creator God, thank you for moments of clarity and peace, as we gaze on the beauty of your world. Lord Jesus, you know our hurts from the past, the things we struggle with, the pain we feel. Forgive us, that we are sometimes too fearful to see the possibilities ahead. Help us have times of stillness in which we find refreshment and inspiration. May we make the most of each day granted. Holy Spirit, grant us courage to step out into the next phase of our lives, whatever that might look like, for we trust in you, Amen.

Blog 59: A House Full of Feathers!

19th July 2021

Expressing loss – a dog's way

I was away for a few days last week, which I loved, and my son looked after our handsome dog Gabriel. I am grateful to him, and others who walked Gabriel when I was absent.

My son was telling me what a good dog he had been, until I got in the door. In the hour he had been away, Gabriel decided to say he was fed up, and ripped a pillow to shreds, leaving a mountain of feathers everywhere. He didn't look remotely concerned about this, as you can see. I think it was just his way of saying he wanted company!

For those who have experienced loss of some kind, it can be difficult to put into words how that feels – an ache in the soul, a lethargy, a heaviness. It is the feeling that is with you first thing in the morning, and last thing at night.

Grieving can cause us to do different things – not always to rip up a pillow, but to decide not to go out, to put off replying to a letter, to want to break things! Sometimes the emotional cost of choosing to do something difficult or new, can seem overwhelming.

We all cope with these in different ways. Sometimes we talk to an understanding friend. Sometimes we binge watch Netflix, just to distract ourselves from the pain. Sometimes we just want to be walking at a beach, or just alone with God, pouring out our soul.

Where we can, it is good to choose healthier options to express anger, loss and pain. We seek to give our regrets and guilt to God, over things we

Colour Section

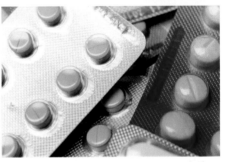

might have wished to be otherwise. We ask for cleansing, and a gradual coming to terms with what happened. Sometimes we shout at God 'why' – because we find it all hard to understand. And we pray for peace in our souls, and strength to tackle the new day in a holistic way.

A verse that has been speaking to my heart recently is from Isaiah 26: 'You will keep in perfect peace, the one who is focused on you, because he trusts and takes refuge in you.' Sometimes when we are hurting, the temptation is to withdraw or to question. These are a healthy part of the process, but we pray that gradually through the ebb and flow dance of grief, that we begin to find a deeper and lasting peace.

> Gracious God, Creator of all, thank you that in the beauty of this world, the shade of a tree or the refreshment of a cool breeze, we are reminded of your presence. Lord Jesus, you wept at the death of your friend Lazarus, and you know the shock and pain of bereavement. Thank you that you weep with us. Holy Spirit, in the midst of our loss, help us to find safe ways to express our heartache (that doesn't involve feathers!) Thankyou for our beautiful pets, and may we always treat them well. We thank you for the interconnectedness of all things, and pray for the gift of peace and a sense of belonging for all who cry to you this day, Amen.

Blog 60: Starfish Bring us Hope!

26th July 2021

God speaks to us every day!

Sometimes I question what my purpose is. I wonder if God can really use me, I am so flawed and feel so small. Can God ever use me to make any kind of difference?

Beaches are a place which encourage me to ponder and to pray. I wrestle with my dreams, and the difference between them and the reality of my situation. Sometimes

I despair, because I want to help others know the reality of God's love in Christ, but I make mistakes, say the wrong thing, and then pray for God to remake me, so I am more loving, thoughtful, considerate. I have such along way to go, as I feel a bit worn down by the experiences I have had in life.

I had the privilege of walking on Luskentyre beach on Harris this month, and when all this heavy stuff was going on in my soul, I saw this gorgeous starfish. And I remembered the starfish story. The synopsis is that some one was throwing stranded starfish into the water, and some one said why do that, there are so many on the beach. You won't be able to help them all. And the person throwing them into the water said, 'It will make a difference for this one.'

We have dreams of making a difference in this world, inspiring change, supporting people on tough days. But the reality is on many days, we are grumpy and on hold, waiting to get through to an energy company, or frustrated that no one in the family seems to be able to pick their clothes up off the floor. There are so many frustrations and distractions each day.

However, God spoke to me through that starfish. If you help just one person, then that is enough. I can stop worrying about the things I can't do, and just be thankful for small things I can do. Mother Theresa said, 'We can do no great things, only small things with great love.'

In Matthew 25:31-46 Jesus famously talks about how just to give food to the hungry, or to give a thirsty person a drink, to show a stranger hospitality, to clothe the naked, or to visit some one in prison, makes a difference.

Even just doing what might seem like an insignificant action, can cause a positive ripple effect for others. So we persevere in faith.

> Gracious God, you encourage us and give us hope, when we question our purpose, and what our life is about. You remind us that even faith the grain of a size of a mustard seed can make a difference. Lord Jesus, please take our offerings, however flawed they are, and use them for your glory. Thank you that every starfish matters, every act of kindness and grace brings your kingdom closer. Holy Spirit, liberate us from worry about what we haven't achieved, and help us to get up each morning, open to your leading, of maybe blessing just one person this day. By your mercy, hear our prayers, Amen.

Blog 61: The Gift of Water . . .

3rd August 2021

Reflective bliss

In Glasgow we often don't appreciate water. It pours from the sky when it is least wanted, breaking your umbrella, soaking through your jacket, and making your feet cold and soggy. Only the reflection of street lights in puddles make it bearable!

Yet the gift of water is amazing, whether it is the gurgling of a stream, the stillness of a loch, or the rhythm of the waves in the ocean. There is something so profoundly cleansing about being immersed in water, experiencing the spray of a waterfall or the waves on a beach.

Swimming gives it a new dimension. To be at one with the water, for your limbs to be working in a rhythm that enables you to move forward, is quite remarkable. I travel slowly, but it is like being home, maybe a womb like experience, with a profound sense of connection to the water.

Wild swimming is the most magical of all, swimming with midges and swallows, clouds and skies, rocky shorelines, and ever changing expanses of blue, black and deep green.

We are so blessed to have such wonderful opportunities to be at peace with nature. We need to be wise as to how we practise, but the freedom of swimming outside is so liberating and full of bliss.

The bible speaks about the majesty of creation, and God's power even over the ocean. In Psalm 93:4 it says in the Passion translation,

> The raging waves lift themselves over and over, high above the ocean's depth, yet at the sound of your voice they are stilled.

When swimming through the waves, to remember the length and width and depth of God's love for us, can also speak to us in a powerful way. God's love reaches us like the profusion of waves, cleansing our souls and healing our hurts, restoring our perspective, as we lose ourselves in the landscape.

> Gracious God, there is something so elemental in being immersed in water, experiencing all the richness of colours and sensations, being rocked by the sea, or inspired by white beaches and azure waters. Thank you for the wonder of your creation, the cycle of seasons, the pull of the moon, the rhythm of the tides. Lord Jesus, you taught people on the shore, you travelled by boat, and you demonstrated that you could quieten the wind and still the storm. Help us have a healthy reverence for your creation. And may your Holy Spirit heal our wounds, soothe our souls, and invigorate our spirits, as we experience the life giving qualities of water! Amen.

Blog 62: Poignant Celebrations

10th August 2021

Joy intermingled with sadness round the edges

I feel so very privileged to celebrate my son's birthday at the weekend. It was a lovely day, of being able to meet up with some family and friends. After so many days of not being able to meet because of all the covid restrictions, it is so appreciated to see real people again, and to talk and catch up. See the photo of Andrew with our dog Gabriel in the colour section.

The things that is tough though, is all the empty spaces. There are so many people missing for one reason or another, it was a little sad around the edges. It is such a mixed feeling of thanksgiving, but also of a realisation that things have changed, and they are not going to go back to where they were.

When you are grieving, this realisation seems to come back a thousand times. You think you know, that you understand, but then the loss of your loved ones take you unawares yet again. Your heart becomes immersed in old memories, the way it used to be, and for better or worse, it all feels so different and disorientating. The meaning is deeper, but somehow also more remote.

In Matthew 5:4 Jesus said, 'Blessed are those who mourn, for they will be comforted.'

At times however, I don't think those who mourn feel very blessed, rather just tearful, confused and exhausted! Yet the thing is, when we are at the end of ourselves, then that is when we rely more heavily on God, when we cry to him for help, every moment of the day, and truly learn to shelter under the shadow of his wing. It takes all our energy just to rest in his love, and pray for healing. And we know that God never forsakes us. God us so patient and so merciful.

For anyone whose heart is sore and hurting, may you know the love of God enfolding you, and his healing grace, and the hope of things one day getting better. And may we all persevere meantime.

> Gracious God, you watch over us with your angels, you provide for us with such tender care, and sometimes we feel guilty for questioning or being sad. Lord Jesus Christ, thank you that you know your sheep, and you love us even when we groan or grumble that our life is tough. Please lift from us that need to pretend we are ok – yes to give thanks, but to acknowledge also that the ache is still there. Holy Spirit, comfort us, strengthen us, and help us to smile even through our tears, for you say that all will be well. May we trust this promise, Amen.

Blog 63: Anger and Advocacy!

14th August 2021

Let's be angry!

At times in today's world, the danger is that we can feel a little numb, a little detached. Sometimes however, we can allow ourselves to feel – to hear another person's story, and in our imagination to feel we are going through it with them, and to identify with their emotions. It could be listening to the person on the train, or a magazine article, some words from the family next door, or a person on the other side of the globe.

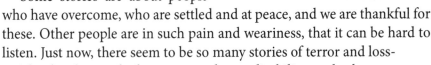

Some stories are about people who have overcome, who are settled and at peace, and we are thankful for these. Other people are in such pain and weariness, that it can be hard to listen. Just now, there seem to be so many stories of terror and loss-

The family in which some one has a disability, and whose support services have been cut because of the pandemic, people who have become more isolated and lost skills and confidence.

The prisoners, languishing in prison, although they have done nothing wrong – people like the Chinese Christian Gao Zhisheng, whose work as a human rights lawyer has resulted in him disappearing in 2017, and he has not been seen since.

And we think of the terrified in Afghanistan, as the Taliban reassert control, the cries of the vulnerable, of women and children fleeing from the brutality and lawlessness of their rule.

How do we respond to these heartbreaking situations. Well maybe, just maybe, we should be angry! We should be angry that people with disabilities and mental health issues seem to be at the bottom of the pile in our society. We should be indignant that human rights lawyers, who courageously speak out for others, can disappear with so many people turning a blind eye. We should be furious that in so many lands, the rights of women and children are non existent.

To be healthy, we cannot focus on all these issues all the time. However to pretend they are not happening, is not the answer either.

As we listen to the cries of these individuals, we should be angry that they suffer so much, and so many do so little. But hopefully it is not the kind of anger that breaks dishes, but rather the kind of anger that we ask God to channel into a constructive energy for advocacy and action.

In Ephesians chapter 4 verse 26, it says 'in your anger, do not sin.' We are allowed to be angry – it is what we do with it that matters. Jesus himself was angry – about the hypocrisy of the Pharisees, or the greed of the money changers in the temple. So he spoke out against that which was wrong.

In Proverbs 31:8-9 it says: 'Speak up for those who cannot speak for themselves, for the rights of all who are destitute'. Part of our calling as Christians, as human beings, is to speak for those who cannot speak for themselves, or those who are not being listened to.

When we are touched by what has happened to some one, and have become indignant, whether it is the plight of the homeless, the story of the woman who has been human trafficked, or the lonely person in a hospital bed, may we channel these feelings of sadness and frustration into something good, to lobby for funding, for advocacy, for change. It might only be the words of a prayer, or writing to our MP, or giving to a charity, but every little helps.

> Gracious God, we remember the roar of Aslan in C.S. Lewis' novels, conveying the power and majesty of God. You are the God of justice, and you long for justice and fairness. Yet on this earth so many suffer – trauma, ill treatment, sexual exploitation and brutality. Forgive us for the times we turn away. Lord Jesus, help us be angry when another human being is treated without dignity or respect. And may your Holy Spirit helps us channel that anger wisely, to pray, to give, to be advocates for those on trouble. Give us energy to do this, and to be courageous in seeking to make this a more just world, Amen.

Blog 64: The Silence Between the Notes

28th August 2021

The significance of pause

It could have been the composer Debussy or Mozart that said that 'music is the space between the notes'. This quotation often recurs in my thoughts, in the midst of busy and pressured days, full of conversations, things to do, places to be.

Life seems a little bewildering just now, full of adjustments to the latest information and recommendations re the covid pandemic. We also are trying to come to terms with losses of so many kinds, during lockdown, in our society, in our life stories. And so our thoughts swirl with regrets, sadnesses, information and possibilities. Often we seem to speak fast to convey the vast amount going on in our heads.

And so this quotation really helps me, that the music can somehow be the space between the notes – what is of significance, can be the timing of the silence. I like the fact that the intervals in pieces of music are called 'rests'. That makes perfect sense to me!

Especially as we move through this time of pandemic, there are many profound questions as to how we should live. And there is a movement towards less frenetic activity, more reflection and quiet appreciation.

Often we discover meaning not just in the moment, but in the time to reflect afterwards. That is when significance deepens, and the experience can be processed and absorbed.

In music, literature and art, so much seems discordant and noisy, exploring extremes, rather than the exquisite tapestry of light and shade in tone and subtlety.

I love the words from Psalm 55:6: 'Oh that I had the wings of a dove. I would fly away and be at rest.'

It would be such a blessing to have these moment of rest and reflection in every day, and in the rhythm of our week. When we live in a hurry, we might seem to get more done, but we lose part of ourselves. We need moments to breathe, to appreciate, to find space.

As we go into a new session of school and church, may we not go back to old ways of haste and hustle, a scramble to fit everything in. Instead, may we be more selective, asking God for his leading. May we have times to reflect and to pray, to receive the meaning and inspiration of experiences and encounters, and to savour them, and to let them shape our understanding and our being.

> Gracious God, Creator of all things, we are told that when you created the universe, the seventh day was a day of rest, when you saw that what was done, was good. However we understand this, we know that times of rest need to be built into the fabric of our lives, times of quiet, of insight of appreciation. Lord Jesus, you often left your disciples and friends, to go to a quiet place to pray. Holy Spirit teach us to ensure that in the regular rhythm of our lives, there are times to rest, to pray, to reflect and to be creative. May times of silence enrich and bless our souls, to deepen our understanding, and to strengthen and energise us for the the rest of life. Grant us that quiet wisdom which illuminates all things, Amen.

Blog 65: A 'Wheelie' up a Hill!

6th September 2021

Exhilaration!

In the traffic the other day, I saw a teenager riding his bike, doing a wheelie up a hill. I have to say it wasn't what he was meant to be doing I am sure, and it didn't look that safe. But what I noticed was the sheer joy and exhilaration on his face. He was so loving it!

In these days of pandemic, sometimes it feels as if everything is grey. It is round after round of changing regulations, new interpretations and constant adaptions. It is necessary but so wearisome.

God wants to bring us seasons of joy. The sheer excitement and enjoyment of that boy on the bike, reminded me of the enjoyment we seem to have lost as a society, and as a church. We are so worn down by uncertainty, fear and suffering and isolation.

A passage I keep going back to just now is Revelation chapter 2, where John writes to the church in Ephesus. He says they have worked hard and persevered, but he says in verse 4 that the one thing that he holds against them, is that they have forsaken their first love.

Maybe we remember how we felt when we first came to faith, our amazement at being loved by God, at being forgiven because of the cross, being accepted into God's family. It is the kind of good news that you think will make you smile for a life time.

Yet over time that joy and thankfulness get eroded by sadness, disappointment, suffering, conflict. At times, we just seem to be going through the motions, surviving each day, rather than living.

I think that God has something better for us. He wants us to come and sit with him, to have our empty cups filled to overflowing with his healing love and grace, so that we are brought back to life, in all its richness and fullness, so we can have moments of rejoicing and joy. I think it can be a slow process, a time of questioning, of erratic moods and much processing. Yet we pray for God to bless his people once more, with that enthusiastic joy in the gospel, and that he would once more breathe new life into us. If only we could know a fraction of the exuberance of a boy on a bike!

Gracious God, forgive us that we become so burden and worn down by cares, that we can be in danger of becoming grey people, worried about many things. Lord Jesus, remind us of your life giving presence, lift our burdens from us, and put them at the foot of the cross. And then having relinquished all that holds us back, may we know the freedom of your Spirit, so we might smile once again, so others might see your life in us, Amen.

Blog 66: A Wistful Emptiness

9th September 2021

Anniversaries and birthdays of those no longer with us

Today would have been Colin's birthday. The date is etched in my soul forever. But what happens when the person is no longer here? For most people, it is just another date in the calendar – of no special significance. Yet for the people left behind, you are marking the date with the key person missing. There is no one there to open the cards and blow out the candles, There is such a mixture of emotions, sadness, thanksgiving, guilt and a longing for things to be otherwise.

Listening to other people's experiences of loss, the guilt of remembering a significant date, is that other people think you should have moved on by now. As the years go by, in some ways, part of you does process things differently, but I think there is still a feeling of profound sadness.

In some situations of grief, feelings are exacerbated by the circumstances of a loss. Very often people choose not to talk much about these, as they can be distressing, and as a society maybe we need to make more space for people to talk more honestly about the messiness of it all.

At the risk of repeating myself, I find it hard to come to terms with what happened with Colin, as it was so unjust, and involved so much suffering, over decades. His head injury led to a long term degeneration through poorly controlled epilepsy. It was hideously painful to witness.

My consolation comes from my faith, that even in the darkest, most bleak and challenging days, God was with us. God blessed Colin with the knowledge that he was loved, even when nothing made any sense.

In Psalm 86:15 it says: 'You, Lord are a compassionate and gracious God, slow to anger, and abounding in love and faithfulness.'

I understand when people question where God is, when something awful is happening in their life, the illness of a child, a gradual loss of faculties, a painful treatment. Watching someone you love suffer is excruciating.

Yet in the most tearful circumstances, there can be a moment of lucidity, a glance of understanding, a loving connection, that can be transformative. And the power of prayer to help find meaning and hope can never be underestimated.

I want to write to encourage people to know no one is alone, even when we have bad days, or when we question, or when it all seems too much. We need to find people we can trust to talk to, even if it is to say the same thing for 100 times. There are some days when that is just what it takes.

> Gracious God, on the outside all looks well, but you see into our hearts – the painful memories, the regrets, the lament – why did it have to happen that way, why did that loved one suffer so much? Lord Jesus, you understand us, for you suffered at the hands of others, when it didn't need to be like that, and you come alongside us with compassionate eyes and cascades of grace. Holy Spirit, lift from us our pain and grief, and help us remember the moments of beauty and trust and love, that transformed even the hardest times. And on days like today, bring healing and a sense of peace, Amen.

Blog 67: A Vision of Harmony!

14th September 2021

Patterns of light

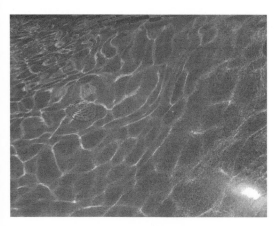

I have been so blessed to have had some time out with family in a sunny place. I realise how very much I have missed opportunities just to rest and be, in a warm climate.

I have especially enjoyed the light here, the amazing variety of colours in the sunsets, and last night the moon reflecting its silver glow across the expanse of the ocean. The bright luminous path in the sea in the starry night was wondrous.

(not my picture, but this was the idea!)

The ripples of light in the water, as I have been swimming, have also been mesmerizing. I have felt harmonious with the water and the air, as new patterns and ripples appear in a pool, or you become one with the rhythms of the waves in the sea.

The wonder of these experiences have been so good for my soul. For a short while I have put to one side images of conflict, poverty and distress, and I feel at peace with nature, and the Creator of all things. It has reminded me of my desire to be in harmony with God, to be at one with Christ, to just rest in God's love.

I used to think that this was selfish, but now I understand that these moments of connection refresh my soul, for the days ahead. Finding time to refuel in the pandemic was strangely difficult, because although there was more time, at times I had to fight a sense of claustrophobia and sadness. I think for many people, the pandemic left us all more isolated, and not able to process our grief in community. So being able to travel has reminded me of that sense of freedom and space and connection.

Ultimately, one of the most beautiful Bible passages about harmony is in Revelation 22:1-3,

> The angel showed me the river of the water of life, as clear as crystal, flowing from the throne of God and of the Lamb, down the middle of the great street of the city. On each side of the river stood the tree of life, bearing 12 crops of fruit. And the leaves of the trees are for the healing of the nations.

I love John's vision of the future, where people are with God, full of praise and worship. It seems no surprise that there is water, clear as crystal, at the centre of the city, bringing healing and beauty and life to all, for the leaves of the trees are to bringing healing to the nations. That spiritual refreshment offers possibilities of transformation for all. Vision such as this brings us strength and hope for the journey ahead.

> Gracious God, our Creator, you have created a world of intricate patterns of light and shade, and of jaw dropping moments of revelation and connection. We worship you, grateful for possibilities of harmony, when the lion and the lamb lie down together. Lord Jesus, in you all things are held together, as the forgiveness you offer through the cross, brings an invitation to reconciliation for all. There are times in this life when pride, grief and violence seem overwhelming. But when we look to you, you remind us of the truth of who you are, and we are reassured and find peace. Through your Holy Spirit, inspire us to work towards healing and harmony even amongst the brokenness, and grant us a clarity of vision to energise us each day, Amen.

Blog 68: Guarding our Hearts

21st September 2021

Keeping them tender

There is so much which feels overwhelming. The effects of the pandemic continue on, the winter is round the corner, the health services seem over stretched and under resourced.

In the midst of this, if you are sitting with chronic illness, living with trauma, or grieving, there is another dimension to things, with feelings of frustration, helplessness and isolation. We can be bewildered, tired and hurting, and so we protect ourselves by putting up barriers to prevent further pain or heartache.

The problem with this is, that the solution becomes worse than the initial issue. We end up becoming numb, locked inside ourselves, unwilling to venture out, and reluctant to trust. It might keep us safe in the short term, but longer term it actually imprison us.

So what do we do? If we are in a caring profession, how can we keep loving, even when we are close to burn out? If we are in difficult relationships, how do we care for people, who we do not easily relate to?

I really wish I had the answer. A verse that is an anchor however is found at Proverbs 4:23: 'Above all else, guard your heart, for it is the wellspring of life.' See the little illustration in the colour section, first page bottom right.

We need to know that our heart, our emotional wellbeing is precious. Sometimes if we have experienced loss or hurt, whether that is in relationship breakdown or death, we get lost in a maze of feelings of questioning, an emotional paralysis and deep ache that oscillate in intensity and can incapacitate us. Our hearts seem broken, and no longer able to function.

I believe that God heals the broken hearted, but it can be quite a long, turbulent process. At times we seem in danger of getting stuck. It is so hard to be patient, and to trust. Sometimes we need time out, to be able to find the support we need to recover, and to know that this is ok.

So we seek to guard our hearts, to make decisions not to over extend what we are trying to do. We need to ask God to keep us from temptation, to slow us down and to give us wisdom, to show us how to live. And I think living a life of prayer is key, for if we know how much we are loved by God, then that loving relationship breathes new life into us each morning, and gives us courage to love that the day ahead. And that is all we need.

> Gracious God, some days we feel empty, rejected or alone. The temptation is to bury our feelings deep down just in order to survive. Forgive us. In Ezekiel chapter 36 you say you will take away our heart of stone, and give us a heart of flesh. Lord Jesus, may your heart beat in ours, and give us courage to feel and to care. Holy Spirit, keep us from temptation, and help us live so closely to Jesus, that we have tender hearts, able to love and be loved. Please fill us with your love every day, and this might somehow then spill over into the lives of others, Amen.

Blog 69: There is Still Good in the World!

25th September 2021

Hope

There are days that seem heavy, when things just don't seem to be working out. It can be little things, a parking fine, the washing machine breaking down, or something more serious, like a misunderstanding with a friend. There are things that frustrate us, worry us, or can just seem like one thing too many. Often it is not just whatever that has happened, that is troubling. It is what it represents, or what we are already trying to deal with, that can make it seem hard. It can be the straw that threatens to break that camel's back.

The danger is that when negative events accumulate, that we lose our sense of perspective, and the world can seem a dark place. It makes us not want to get up in the morning, or to want to escape our responsibilities for a while.

This week was very busy, and I seemed to run from meeting to meeting. One evening, about 8.30pm a young man came to my door, and asked if I had lost anything. I said no – reasonable confidently. Then he gave me my purse back, sealed in a transparent plastic bag. His girlfriend had found it, where I had dropped it, over 5 miles away, and they brought it back to me intact, and out of the kindness of their hearts. They didn't want anything for it, they just wanted to reunite it with its owner.

In the midst of these turbulent days, it is good to be reminded that some people are just really kind. They have no hidden agenda, no selfish motives, they just want to do the right thing. And meeting these people is such a joy, and actually there are so many about. They remind us of the goodness in the world, and that there is always still hope.

In the bible, there are so many stories, where people make mistakes, or are struggling with purpose or loss, and then something brings them a glimpse of more positive possibilities. The Psalms are full of such moments, and a recurring theme is that God's nature never changes. It is so simple and yet powerful, like Psalm 100:5, 'For the Lord is God, his loving kindness is everlasting.' We are so thankful.

> Gracious God, we all have days when we feel down, when so many things go wrong – some are just frustrating, others deeply worrying, and they all deplete our energy. Lord Jesus, when we feel like this, may we remember your unrelenting goodness and grace, and find hope. Thank you for people who quietly show great kindness to others. And when we wonder where these people are, may your Holy Spirit inspire us to be people of grace and care to others. Thank you for all the good in this world, we praise you, Amen.

Blog 70: Waves of Suffering Everywhere

2nd October 2021

Turmoil

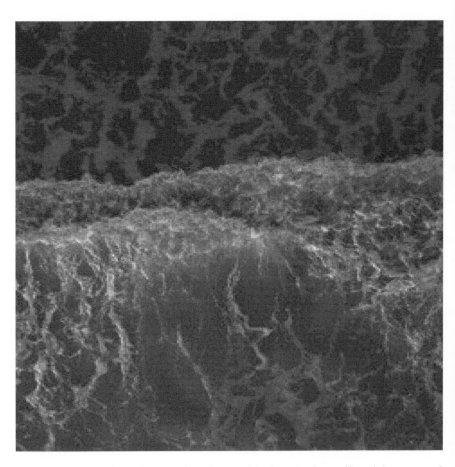

I choose to affirm the good in the world, that God is still real, loving and powerful, that there is still hope. But sometimes to make these statements takes such courage.

In the week where the details of Sarah Everard's death have come to light, it seems that so much is broken, it is hard to ever imagine any kind of repair. Her trust was violated in so many ways it is hard to put into words. That people can be so intentionally cruel and brutal to another human being is terrifying.

I think however that the problem is that this terrible abuse of power, this rape and murder just remind us of the reality of what goes on daily for many people. Whether you are talking about domestic violence or human trafficking, some one choosing to violently exploit and control another human being is all too common. Institutional corruption is endemic in so many places. And we often turn a blind eye. We pretend not to see, we pretend things will get better. And it doesn't.

As a human race, we need to weep over the seemingly unrelenting brutality and violence in our world. We need to pray for it to stop, for us to support charities working in this area, to do what we can to support those affected by it in any way. There are too many children and adults traumatised by abuse and violence.

Jesus said, 'Come to me, all those who are weary, and I will give you rest.' (Matthew 11:28)

When we are tired of putting on a face, being brave, of crying on the inside, we can come to Jesus and be honest, and pour out our hearts to him. In the presence of God, we are safe, and can find shelter and healing. It might just be a first step in a healing process, but in the midst of the overwhelming pain and suffering of the world, it is an essential refuge. Even in the midst of heartbreak and sorrow, God's love for us has never changed.

> Gracious God, you are full of loving kindness and grace, and you created this world to mirror the beauty and harmony of who you are. But we have rebelled and sullied our planet and our relationships, and been exploitative and cruel. Lord Jesus, you who experienced the brutality and callousness of human beings on that Friday of Holy Week, have mercy on our souls. In the ongoing spiritual battle, may we pray for evil to be restrained, and for the vulnerable to be protected. And please can your life giving Holy Spirit bring healing to all who have suffered at the hands of another, so that in time they might trust and heal once more, Amen.

Blog 71 Unexpected Laughter!

9th October 2021

The freedom to laugh like a child!

Laughter can be a great gift, as there can be such freedom in seeing the humour in a situation, and to be able to express that. Laughter can lift your spirits, help release tension and help you see things from a different perspective. It brings feel good endorphins and dopamine into your system.

However I have noticed that there have been seasons where I have been laughing for no obvious reason. Meetings are not always the best place to start laughing, but sometimes if you notice an incongruity or unconscious humour, it can be hard to look serious for too long, however hard you try.

I haven't quite worked it out, but I think my laughter has often been related to my grief and pain. When you are bereaved, you can have all this sadness and tension inside, and somehow this pain can express itself in hysterical laughter. It seems like some kind of release mechanism, to let some of the pain out in a laughter response, that is so deep you often indeed end up in tears. I don't know if this will make sense to anyone else, but it has been my experience, so I just thought I would try to express it. (I also understand if you don't want to sit in a meeting with me!)

I always remember the words in Nehemiah 8:10, 'Do not grieve, for the joy of the Lord is your strength.' The people gathered to hear God's word in Jerusalem that day were sad because of all that had happened in the past, but the joy of being in God's presence helped them to find joy, even then. The people ended up both laughing and crying together.

In Ecclesiastes chapter 3 it says that 'there is a season for everything under the sun' and I think as we cope with the joys and sorrows of life, our body can often respond in unexpected ways. Maybe we need to be patient and understanding, even when we don't fully comprehend. Fortunately this season of unexpected laughter has lessened in frequency and intensity, but every now and again . . .

> Gracious and Eternal God, you are the Giver of every good gift, you are so wise and gracious. In our brokenness, we confess that at time we do not understand ourselves, or why we react the way we do. Lord Jesus, thank you for your mercy, that even with our eccentricities, You look upon us with love. We are humbled and amazed. Whatever we are struggling with just now, may your Holy Spirit heal us, and help us to live life in all its fullness, even with tears and laughter, Amen.

Blog 72: Actively Involved in the Healing Process!

16th October 2021

Participating is hard work!

I am so grateful that healing is such a strong theme in the bible. Whether it is the healing of Hezekiah in 2 Kings 20, or Jesus' amazing healing ministry depicted in the gospels, God loves to heal in body, mind and soul.

I fully recognise the complexity of this topic, as sometimes we pray for people and they don't seem to get better. We don't know why some prayers don't seem to be answered. Maybe sometimes the damage is too great, or the process to get better just too arduous for a human being to bear. We just don't know, and it is distressing and exhausting trying to work it out.

I have been reading a lot recently about healing from trauma, and about finding ways of feeling safe and becoming more whole again. And I am always surprised at how much hard work it is. Working with topics like low self esteem, childhood or adult trauma, anger management etc seems so tough. For example, if for whatever reason, you don't like some one shouting at you. You learn this insight, and what experience caused you to think like this, and to respond like this. Investigation complete, so you think.

However this is actually just the start. For identifying the trauma, then starts you on a path of what you do to cope, what your protective mechanism is, eg to avoid angry people, to withdraw etc. And often the coping mechanism then becomes part of the problem, because it forms an unhealthy pattern of behaviour, a bad habit. So then if there is a loud voice or angry behaviour, you recognise the impact it is having on you, and you then learn to choose to respond differently. You choose to stay in the room, take a deep breath, and give a boundaried answer.

That sounds great in theory, but putting it into practice is exhausting. And putting this into practice with multiple different traumas, makes it complicated and wearisome. It is one step forward and two back.

I am so blessed to have the resources to think this through, and to seek healing. God is so faithful, He never lets us down, and always provides a safe place to ask difficult questions, and to ask for strength to change. The Holy Spirit challenges us, and brings insight, strength to change, and much healing. However we also need to intentionally participate, to face up to difficult memories, and to be open to change. May we all find continued motivation and perseverance to continue on this path.

A verse comes to mind: 'O Lord, you are our Father: we are the clay, and you are our potter, we are all the work of your hand.' (Isaiah 64:8)

We all need to be fashioned, to be willing to change, for the clay to be soft and malleable in the hand of the potter, for something beautiful to be created.

> Gracious Creator God, you see the brokenness in our world, the distorted thoughts, the shattered self image, our doubts and fears, our negative ways of thinking. Heal us we pray, in Jesus' name. And even when it is wearisome, repetitive work, where we need to pause, and choose to respond differently, give us courage. May your Holy Spirit help us let go of destructive and negative ways of thinking, so we can live in freedom, and find the deep and lasting wholeness we seek, in Jesus' name, Amen.

Blog 73: Compassion in Hostile Environments
23rd October 2021

Grace and acceptance towards one another

In recent weeks, there have been many conversations about what is most important in the world. For me, my Christian faith earths me in God's love, Jesus' teaching challenges how I live each day, and His Holy spirit encourages and remakes me. But there is also the wider question about what general qualities are most significant in human relationships, and how to care for our planet. How do we discover and then express this?

We are still in pandemic mode, with so many still getting the covid 19 virus, so many isolating, hospitalised or sadly dying. And the consequences of the backlogs in social care, education and health care especially leading to long waiting lists, lack of resources and shortages of staff. Our society seems fractured, and the pandemic has accentuated and accelerated injustice, isolation and multiple crises. We need many wise people to manage well, to direct resources, and to plan strategically.

However in much planning, there sometimes seems to be a lack of basic humanity and compassion. Soulless bureaucrats have power but are not always listening to people on the ground, as to what is most needed. Fulfilling quotas and keeping to timetables, does not always reflect that we have done our best to listen to the needs of, and to support the individual in front of us. I love this quotation from Henri Nouwen:

> Compassion asks us to go where it hurts, to enter into places of pain, to share in brokenness, fear and confusion and anguish. Compassion challenges us to cry out with those in misery, to mourn with those who are lonely, to weep with those in tears. Compassion requires us to be weak with the weak, vulnerable with the vulnerable, and powerless with the powerless. Compassion means full immersion in the condition of being human.[11]

11 Henri Nouwen, Donald P. McNeill and Douglas A. Morrison, *Compassion: A Reflection on the Christian Life*, Doubleday, New York 1982, 4.

Jesus showed compassion to the sick child, the woman who was ill, the man with leprosy. He spent time with those on the edges of society, the person who collected taxes, who was a rebel, who prostituted themselves for money. Jesus had a heart and a message for all. He offered them a way back to God, to cleansing, forgiveness and a new beginning.

In our society, we have been through so much in recent years, it seems that we are exhausted, at times numb, on automatic pilot. It is easy to think that the wellbeing of others is not our responsibility. However if we follow that model then we create a harsh world where self preservation and convenience are our only concerns.

May we look to God for answers, to the life and ministry of Jesus for our models. 'When Jesus saw the crowds, he had compassion on them, because they were harassed and helpless, like sheep without a shepherd' (Matthew 9:36). May we too show compassion to others, by praying, listening, giving a safe space, and affirming and supporting each other.

> Gracious God, sometimes so much has happened to us, that we become hard hearted, for we are hurting and sorrowful, and we find it hard just to survive. We protect ourselves by covering ourselves with a hard shell. Lord Jesus, look upon us with compassion, and soften our hearts with your abundant and undeserved grace, acceptance and love. Help us know the depth of your care for us, so we in turn can show similar compassion to others. Holy Spirit, each morning, may you fill us with tender love and empathy for others, so we can see them through your eyes, and show compassion, Amen

We think of the lyrics of Graham Kendrick's song 'Beauty for brokeness':

> Friend of the weak, give us compassion we pray,
> melt our cold hearts, let tears fall like rain,
> come change our love from a spark to a flame.

Blog 74: Engaged and Distracted!

1st November 2021

Aching beauty even in times of change and loss

Autumn is a stunning time of year – the varying colours and textures, the sounds of leaves crunching underfoot and the aching beauty of bare branches and naked trees. It is a time that speaks of loss and the inevitability of change.

November is a difficult month for me, and the heaviness of Remembrance seems all too near. The trauma and suffering of military personnel and their families seem tangible.

We seem to cope with trauma and loss in such diverse ways. There are times when we seem numb, when it all seems remote. The coping strategy is to look for distraction from the pain, to watch too many boxed sets, to go to the gym, to eat tubs of ice cream. We do anything not to engage, not to have to feel.

But every now and again, it catches us up, and we feel intensely. It could be a moment in a film, or a message from a friend, or just a word in a sentence, and it brings it all back, so that we crumple and fall apart.

Bessel van der Kolk, cited already on page 14, says:

> Traumatised people chronically feel unsafe in their bodies. The past is alive in the form of gnawing interior discomfort. Their bodies are constantly bombarded by visceral warning signs, and in an attempt to control these processes, they often become expert at ignoring their gut feelings, and in numbing awareness of what is played out inside. They learn to hide from themselves.

This is such a good description of that feeling of numbness. For short periods, it can protect us, as when we are in shock after something terrible has happened. But the danger is that if we stay there too long, that we lose ourselves. And so we need to find the courage to come out and face the pain, however excruciating that can be. Noticing and acknowledging the impact of trauma, is the first step. Often we need to go through this process in company with a trauma informed therapist, or grief counsellor, who can help people to work out what is going on, and to create a safe space to heal.

There are times when we need distraction from the reality of life, the pain and cruelty are too overwhelming. But at other times, we need to have the courage to engage with our story, and the impact it has had on us. At these times of honest engagement, then we are open to finding the long, meandering road to wholeness.

The words of Psalm 32:7 reminds us that in God's presence we find safety. 'You are my hiding place You will protect me from trouble, and surround me with songs of deliverance.' With God, we can find that safe place to be honest, to lament, and to begin to trust and to find the wholeness we seek. And so we take that first step . . .

> Gracious God, you see what happens to your precious children, that we hurt others and get hurt, that we experience loss, and disappointment and trauma. Sometimes we hide, and pretend everything is ok, just to protect ourselves from possibilities of danger. Lord Jesus, you show us such acceptance and love, that your presence is a safe place for us to be to be honest, so we can pour forth our hurts and our wailings. In your perfect timing, may we find courage to be truthful, even when that is uncomfortable and strips our souls bare. May your Holy Spirit help us find pathways through pain, to healing and trust and new growth, Amen.

Blog 75: Helicopters Overhead!

7th November 2021

The sound of rotors

Over the last three weeks, the characteristic noise from the skies has been the sound of helicopters above. Living in Glasgow, where COP26 has been held, the security for the conference on climate justice has involved so many, with every precaution taken to keep people safe.

I have read some of the papers about climate justice, but wanted to understand more, so I went to Glasgow Green last Saturday to hear the speakers, and to get a better sense of what they key issues are, and what we can do. I seem to learn better in person, than just by reading.

Vanessa Nakate

The street protest in Glasgow involved over 100,000 people even in the pouring rain and strong winds. At Glasgow Green there was a great variety of speakers from many different organisations. One of the most powerful was Vanessa Nakate from Uganda. She spoke about the devastation happening in Uganda from uncharacteristic storms, and the impact on the global south from changing weather patterns. Another speaker from the Marshall Islands spoke of her concern than unless global warming is kept to 1.5 degrees, that these islands will become completely submerged by rising sea levels, possibly in the next 20 years. Hearing the stories of these speakers, and many others, brought the urgency of climate justice home.

There is so much to be done. We can lobby our governments to keep the promises they make on emissions, forestation and climate initiatives. We can pray for governments and international corporations to put ethical environmental concerns before profits. We can campaign for educational initiatives to inform and to inspire change.

I have also been challenged about how I live each day. Can I use refillable products from shops like Locovare, to reduce plastic waste? Can I use locally produced products more? Can I lead a simpler life, buying less, using my car less often, perhaps eating less red meat? So many questions. I have started even just a few wee steps to change, and I guess if we all start, then this is how we make progress.

I remember the opening words of Psalm 19: 'The heavens are telling of the glory of God, the heavens declare the work of his hands. Day after day they pour forth speech, night after night reveals knowledge.'

We have been called to be good stewards of this gorgeous planet, with such rich ecosystems, such gorgeous colours and forms. There is enough for everyone, if we are willing to be less greedy, and to share well. Are we?

> Gracious God, you have created the heavens and the earth, and they tell of your glory and goodness every day. But we the people of the earth mine, destroy and exploit the resources of this earth, to make money, to wield power, to exploit those who live on the edges. Lord Jesus Christ, have mercy upon us. Holy Spirit burn away our disinterest and complacency, and grant us tender hearts, which care, and desire to be thoughtful stewards of this earth and her people. Give us self discipline to live differently, courage to change, and inspiration to make a difference, Amen.

Blog 76 Remembrance!

13th November 2021

Remembrance Sunday

Each year we have the painful but very necessary opportunity to remember those who have given their life in conflict and war, those who have been injured or maimed, and to think of their families. It is so important that we do this, as it is too easy for us as a society to forget. We remember all wars, from the first world war in 1914-1918, till the present; wreaths of poppies are laid at memorials (see fourth page of colour section).

This year, many people are talking about how poignant it is especially for veterans who have fought in Afghanistan. After the sudden withdrawal of troops in August this year, the Taliban quickly swept back to power, and there are many people who are living in fear, women scared to go out, families without food. We think of the many who helped troops – interpreters and humanitarians, who are desperate to escape, fearful of reprisals, and worried for their safety, and of their relatives. It is tragic.

One journalist spoke to veterans from Afghanistan living in Canada, where they were talking about how painful it is to remember. There are so many unhealed traumatic memories causing flashbacks and nightmares, it is hard to re-engage. However we do so to remember those who gave their lives, and those who still live today. We are all privileged to do so, but it is so agonising and at times almost unbearable. So we choose to remember in different ways.

At Remembrance, I think of Colin, who was so proud to serve, and to try to make the world a better place. But the cost was so great, that it is is heartbreaking. At times it seems almost too distressing to contemplate.

When thinking of the pain of remembering, it reminds me of the last supper, where Jesus told his friends to remember him, by sharing bread – which was his body broken for them, and wine – his blood shed for them. He told the disciples that everytime they eat and drink, it was to remember him. The first time they did this after Jesus' death and ascension must gave been so emotional, tearful, for their sense of his loss was so great. Yet it also brought them comfort, for through the sacrament, they experienced the nearness of his presence. And so we continue to remember today . . .

Remembering is painful, but we pray for all those affected by war, that somehow Remembrance Sunday might help. It hopefully reminds people that they are not alone, that what they did was worth something, that they have significance. We hope that in the silence, even in the moments where there are memories too deep to be expressed in words, that they might know the comfort of a God who cares. And also a feeling of solidarity with millions around the world.

> Gracious God, you are the eternal God, our refuge, and underneath are the everlasting arms. In the midst of painful and sometimes excruciating memories, may we nestle in your arms. Prince of Peace, our Lord Jesus Christ, you call for justice and reconciliation, but at times we cannot forgive ourselves never mind others. Please be with all those haunted by what they have seen and done, and bring your healing love, and your peace. For those living under threat today, may they find a place of sanctuary. Holy Spirit be at work on this Remembrance Sunday, to help veterans know that they are seen, their pain acknowledged, and that somehow there is still a hope and a future for them. In Jesus' name, Amen.

Blog 77: Overload – One Thing too Many!

20th November 2021

Christmas is coming

My goodness, I can't believe that Christmas seems so close! Decorations are up in house windows, shops and streets. The lights are symbols of hope in dark days, and in many ways are welcome, however early it seems.

However I think there are mixed feelings for those who mourn, a desire to look forward with hope, alongside an awareness of the strain of missing a loved one, and feeling that no one else understands. You can be making plans, but some one us missing, the landscape feels different everything jars, if there is a Christmas card that never arrives, an empty chair, and a deep feeling of loss. Outwardly things might look very similar, but inside the feeling is different. People are often doing their best to help, and you don't want to hurt their feelings. So you try hard to go through the motions, whilst nursing a broken heart.

We know the comforting bible verses inside out – 'God is close to the broken hearted, and saves those who are crushed in spirit' (Psalm 34:18), and sometimes it is ok to stop filling our time with being busy, to pause, to let the hurt bubble up, and to weep. It is honest, and that is often when we feel God the closest, when we tell him of our pain.

When we try to push the pain down, and don't acknowledge it, that's when we go into overload. It means that we overreact to unforeseen frustrations, pressures at work, the unexpected bill, the driver who cuts out in front of us, the ill judged words of a friend. Sometimes it can just be one thing too many which sends us into a tailspin. We are trying so hard, it doesn't take much to derail us.

If we are hurting this Christmas, for whatever reason, a broken relationship, ill health, disrupted plans, the loss of a loved one, it is ok to take time to be with God and to cry out to him. He notices our every tear, and brings us comfort and grace, reminding us that we are never alone, and that our cries are heard. If we are able to slow down, and talk to God about our sadnesses, he can minister to us, and this is when we find the strength and the peace we need.

> Gracious God, you search and you know us, before even a word is on our tongue, you know what is on our hearts. Forgive us for the times we pretend everything is alright, as sometimes we deceive even ourselves. We get so overloaded and so frustrated, short tempered and upset. Lord Jesus, come alongside us, and speak your word of truth, the truth that sets us free. Help us to know it is ok to be real with you, and with trusted loved ones. Help us through the power of your Holy Spirit, to find safe places to lament and to be real, so that we can find that healing and centredness we yearn for. Grant peace to all who are anxious about facing Christmas by themselves, and may they find that your love will encircle and strengthen them, Amen.

Blog 78: A Grief that Feels Like Fear

3rd December 2021

No words describe it . . .

There is a new film out about C. S. Lewis, 'The most reluctant convert'. I would love to see it, and to find out more about C.S. Lewis' life. Lewis was born in Belfast, fought in world war one, lectured at Oxford University, and was a friend of J.R.R. Tolkien. He was a fascinating man, who went through a long period of his life as an atheist. However in 1929 he became a Christian. He wrote many books of insights about Christianity, as well as the famous Narnia series. He also wrote more philosophical books such as *The Problem of Pain*.

Later in his life he married Joy Davidman Gresham, and sadly she developed cancer, and died in 1960. Lewis then wrote a slim book *A Grief Observed* about how it felt to lose someone. It is very intense, and I want to share a quotation from the beginning of the book:

> No one ever told me that grief felt so much like fear. I am not afraid, but the sensation is like being afraid. The same fluttering in the stomach, the same restlessness, the yawning. I keep on swallowing.

> At other times it feels like bring mildly drunk or concussed. There
> is a sort of invisible blanket between the world and me. I find it
> hard to take in what anyone says. Or perhaps hard to want to take
> it in. It is so uninteresting. Yet I want the others to be about me. I
> dread the moments when the house is empty. If only they would
> talk to one another, and not to me.

I find this quotation so deeply moving, such an accurate description of
the physical sensations of grief, a mixture of detachment and fear. And he
speaks of that restlessness, where you cannot settle or concentrate, you
want company, but you don't have the focus to listen properly. It is like
living a vortex of contradictions, that are confusing and disorientating.
You wonder if things will ever feel different.

In John 11:35 it says 'Jesus wept'. He wept over the death of his friend
Lazarus, and was deeply moved by the grief and bewilderment of Mary
and Martha. His soul was troubled at all that was taking place.

Jesus understands our grief, even when it is raw and unsightly, even
when we are sobbing, eyes red and face blotchy. He doesn't turn away,
but sticks with us closer than a brother, holding us in the pain and
questioning and emptiness. The presence of Jesus doesn't solve all our
problems, but his love quietens our soul, and helps us to heal and rest,
and to carry us through sleepless nights of replaying memories and of
lamentation. And so we keep trusting.

> Eternal Father, you look upon us with mercy and grace, especially
> when we feel alone and struggling. We mourn over so many losses,
> some so very raw and others that recur from the past, catching us
> unawares. As we struggle with powerful and difficult emotions,
> Lord Jesus, you come alongside us and weep with us. You sing
> over us, and quieten us with your love, bringing your healing
> lullaby of peace to our exhausted souls. Your Holy Spirit helps us
> not to fear, and carries us through the darkest of nights, enabling
> us to rest. Thank you Lord, Amen.

Blog 79: Hallelujahs – Finding Perspective Through Praise!
11th December 2021

Praise in the darker days

'O come let us worship and bow down, let us kneel before the Lord our Maker' (Psalm 96:6)

At the moment, it feels as if we are all going through every emotion – Christmas approaching, a new virus variant, so many stories of tragedy, local and international. These are such turbulent days.

I think at times it can all feel overwhelming. For people who have experienced trauma and bereavement, it can be even more unsettling, because there are so many triggers, and so many old wounds are reopened. What can we do, to rediscover our equilibrium when we feel troubled and off balance?

For me, I need to spend time with God, time with his word, time in worship. This reminds me that God is still present, and that his goodness and mercy never fail. Worship reminds me of the bigger picture, helps me remember that I am a child of God and restores my perspective.

The psalms express something of that perspective, people being real, questioning and lamenting. Re-reading this book of prayers and praise can help in days of dismay and weariness.

There are days however when it can be hard to concentrate, and so beautiful praise music can be ideal to find connection with God, and opportunities for worship.

On days when we hunger for God's presence, music like 'Nothing else' by Cody Carnes, can remind us of the beauty and wonder of God's presence. If we are experiencing a time of waiting and uncertainty, 'While I wait' by Lincoln Brewster can transport is into the presence of God. If we are experiencing sorrow, 'When the tears fall' by Tim Hughes is so deeply moving. The song 'Broken Hallelujahs' expresses that we can worship, even when we don't understand and are hurting. We might not find all the answers, but we find a God who cares.

Sometimes we think that in order to pray or to praise God we need the right words, or we need a certain amount of faith. But Jesus calls us to come as we are, with faith even the size of a grain of mustard. He accepts our faltering words, and mumbling groans. And so we are thankful.

> Merciful God, we know that we are created in your image, to live in relation to you, to receive your love, and to share it with others. Yet sometimes we get hurt, and are sorrowful and disillusioned, and we are in danger of retreating inside ourselves. Lord Jesus, you understand the pain of human existence, and you came to save us from our sins, to bring healing, to set us free. When we are struggling, may we ask your Holy Spirit to help us reconnect to you, to sing our Hallelujahs, even when they are just a whisper echoing down the corridors of eternity. Even when we are crawling, and on our knees, may we worship and trust, and somehow gain perspective, to know that we are heard and loved, for you are faithful. Enfold us in your love, that we may find peace and strength, Amen.

Blog 80: Putting up the Christmas Tree – Special Memories!

19th December 2021

In the centre of the colour section, there is a photo from about 14 years ago., a photo of Colin and Andrew putting up the Christmas tree. The memories are lovely, because everyone loved putting up the tree – as you can see! We put on Christmas music, found the decorations in the loft, brought everything downstairs and started. Many decorations were made by Andrew, or chosen on a special occasion. There was tinsel everywhere, and the result wasn't always the neatest. As a family it was a fun activity to do together, with food and drink and even some dancing!

I so miss this. Today we bring the box down from the loft, and wonder who has time to untangle the lights, or get new ones. It has become a bit of a chore. There are so many fewer presents, as people are no longer here. It feels as if it has lost its sparkle.

If we have a Christmas with family all around, it is good to give thanks, and to enjoy all the people interactions, all the bustle and noise. If there are small children involved, then appreciate their wonder and even their tantrums!

Quieter Christmases are just different. There is more space to read, and walk and enjoy music. The Christmas tree eventually goes up, although there is a hint of sadness in its branches.

I remember the verse, 'Give thanks in all circumstances, for this is the will of God in Christ Jesus our Lord for you.' (1 Thessalonians 5:18)

There is something about giving thanks when it is busy, there are toys, and visits and laughter and chaos. Yet also giving thanks when Christmas involves fewer people, and less variety and voices. The challenge is to create new rituals and traditions, to form new communities and to find peace.

Gracious God, before your face, generations rise and pass away. Thank you for Christmas, and all the ways that we celebrate the coming of Jesus Christ into this world, the Babe of Bethlehem. We give thanks for the wonder and joy of children, and that they bring this dimension into the day. And we give thanks even when the place settings are empty, and a number of years have gone by. We remember with deep thanksgiving, and we treasure what we have. Holy Spirit touch the lives of all for whom this Christmas is tough, and the loss of a loved one so raw. May we all find comfort, and in time courage to create new traditions, for the sake of our Saviour Jesus Christ, Amen.

Blog 81: Grief Creeping in Round the Edges – Again

27th December 2021

Exhaustion and beauty together (see page 1 of colour section)

Christmas Day is now passed. It is a time of thanksgiving, for people that we have spent time with, gifts exchanged, worship in church – atmospheric and inspiring! So much to appreciate.

Despite my strenuous and best efforts, I still find it hard not to grieve as well. I think that I have lost three close relatives in three years, and there is something about the intensity of that, exacerbated by the restrictions of the pandemic, that just seem hard to overcome. I suspect I need to try less hard, and just let things be. It is exhausting trying to be content.

My parents-in-law loved showing hospitality at Christmas. They would have the flat decorated, their table would look amazing, they loved to cook food, and for people to chat together. There were elegant candles and tiny shiny angels. They were truly convivial people, and they enjoyed creating a welcoming and lovely space.

There is a cliche about loss, that when some one dies, that there is an empty place at the table. For me, it feels so much bigger than that because the table itself has gone. There is a loss of the whole experience, which will never return.

I am so grateful for the patience of God. He lets me be sorrowful when I need to. When I am trying hard to be optimistic, He gives me space to acknowledge my grief. In Matthew 5:4 Jesus says, 'Blessed are those who mourn for they will be comforted'. And in these days of mixed emotions, the presence of God is indeed a solace.

Eternal God, you are so patient and loving when we hurt. Sometimes we try to hard to heal, as it feels as if we should be better by now, that people don't want to listen to our continued sadnesses. We exhaust ourselves trying to be upbeat, and grief creeps back in around the edges. Lord Jesus thank you that you love us as we are, that you are our Emmanuel, the God who is with us. You reach down to us, and enfold us in your love, and let us rest. Holy Spirit we know you transform our souls, in your perfect timing. Meantime, help us just to wait, quietly, patiently, but with the hope that one day things will indeed be better, Amen.

Blog 82: The Weather Forecast Said Rain . . .

28th December 2021

But it was wrong!

This morning, the skies looked overcast and grey, and the weather forecast said it would rain. It didn't look like a day for going out. However, I really felt like some fresh air, so putting on a big rainproof coat and boots, I ventured out, expecting the worst.

The thing was, as I started up a modest hill, all of a sudden the sun started to come out from between the clouds. The colours of the landscape around looked as if they were on fire, with yellows and oranges. And the deep indigo sky reflected in the water, and everything was gorgeous. It was such a clear and awesome view, made the more precious by being completely unexpected. It was a gift!

How often are we put off from doing something, because we are advised it is not a good idea, or it will be too hard, or it is just not possible. However listening to the negativity or advice of others is not always a good idea. It is worth listening to people's insights, but we always need to ask the Holy Spirit to guide us, and help us discern what to do. Sometimes it is worth venturing out, even when it looks like it might rain! There might be amazing experiences that we will miss if we stay in.

There is a weariness and cynicism around in the world, that can weigh us down, and make us question if it is worth bothering. But when we look to Jesus' example, he persevered and kept on loving, even when he faced misunderstanding, opposition and even death. Through the cross, Love overcame all things.

I believe that it is important to keep venturing out, even when we do not know what we might face. In Romans 5, Paul writes about how suffering produces patient endurance, which brings character and hope. Even when things go wrong, God can help us learn things which might help another soul.

Galatians 6:9 is also a timely reminder, 'Let us not grow weary in doing good, for at the right time, we will reap, if we do not give in.' A song from J.J. Heller 'Don't give up too soon' is a gentle reminder of this theme, and worth listening to.

There might be grey days, when we need to stay in and rest. There are days to go forward however, and to keep going, and not give up. For who knows what we will find, if we just keep taking the next step.

> Eternal Father, you are the Creator of all things, and just being in your creation is such a blessing and inspiration, in all weathers. Lord Jesus, I confess sometimes I am easily put off, or discouraged from a new venture or project, because I am scared of all that might go wrong. Yet you set your face towards Jerusalem, even though you faced opposition, as it was the only way to fulfil your purpose. Holy Spirit, help us all to discern what to do, and when. Help us not give up too soon, but through prayer and encouragement, to persevere on our journey, Amen.

Blog 83: Letting Go the Toilet Roll from the Back of the Car! 31st December 2021

Not needed!

Pandemics do strange things to people. We adopt survival habits, which seem a good idea at the time, but don't hold up so well longer term. In the first months of the pandemic, there was a complete panic in society that we were going to run out of toilet rolls, and so many shop shelves were empty. And so I used to keep a packet of toilets rolls in the back seat of the car, so if I met someone who didn't have any, I could offer them a packet. It seemed like a good idea!

However 21 months later, I still have a packet of toilet paper in the back of the car. I know that I don't need them, that in fact no one needs them, but it has been hard to let go. What if there is another shortage?

I think that we have all put strategies in place to help us deal with the pandemic, new patterns of living to seek to keep us and others safe, going out less often, doing our lateral flow tests etc. Many of these patterns are necessary and good.

However for some of our coping strategies, we need to adapt, and to let go. They are no longer relevant – hoarding our favourite food, ordering everything on line, deciding we don't need to catch up with friends the same way. It feels a little as if we are trying to control things, to make things seem better, to try to erase our worries and anxieties.

I love the verses from Jesus in Matthew 6:25 onwards:

> Therefore I tell you, do not worry about your life, what you will eat or what you will drink, or about your body, what you will wear. Is life not more than food, the body more than clothing. Look at the birds of the air, they neither sow nor reap, nor gather into barns, and yet your heavenly Father feeds them. Are you not worth much more than they?'

Do not worry, are words I think we all need to hear, especially as we go into a new year. Sometimes we get frazzled trying to sort things out, trying to envisage what might happen, and to try to prevent it. We so overthink.

God calls us just to trust him, not to prepare for things that haven't yet happened, to put our energy into worrying when we don't know what the future will bring. Our heavenly Father knows us, he knows what we need, and he will provide for us, with grace and care. And so in this year ahead, may we lay aside unhealthy patterns and worries from the past, and find courage to go forward in freedom.

> Gracious God, you give us freedom to choose how we respond to the dilemmas and enigmas of this life. Sometimes we have got stuck in old habits, negative patterns and worries. Lord Jesus, you came into this world to set us free, and to give us life in all its fullness. Holy Spirit give us discernment to let go of unnecessary burdens and habits, and heal us, so we can live in freedom, and make wise choices in the present. As we enter into another year. May we trust you, for your eye is even on the sparrow, and so your love and provision for us is even more wonderful. Thank you Jesus, Amen.

Blog 84: Finding New Paths

8th January 2022

Sloy Dam!

It is amazing how often at the beginning of a new year, we feel compelled to give up bad habits and to embrace new more healthy ones. This week, I was able to try a bit of hill walking, on a beautiful winter day. It was glorious!

However it didn't start like this. It started with the thought, should I really be doing this. Finding the car park to start off with was hard enough, never mind the right path. The signs were far from clear, and it was only watching the wee group of people ahead, that gave me a clue which was the right gate to go through to start off. It was just a bit disorientating.

After I came back however, I had chatted to other people, consulted a map, and got my bearings much better. Now it has become familiar territory, and much easier to contemplate doing again.

It reminded me that doing things for the first time, is often pretty scary. However well prepared we are, we have to interpret new information, process our enviroment and find our direction. It takes energy and courage.

For people who are traumatised or grieving, there are many things that we need to learn to do, to be self aware and to have confidence to explore – whether it is making a choice, going out with friends or moving house. There are decisions that need to be made, and often we need to have courage to take that first step.

> Your word is a lamp to my feet, and a light to my path.
>
> (Psalm 119:105)

Knowing God's word helps us to honour him in our decision making, and gives us a moral compass. His Holy Spirit guides us as to what might harm us or bless us, and this helps us make the best decisions, even when they are scary or new. We give thanks that we are never alone, and that God guides us and helps us venture out on new paths.

> Eternal Father, we often are anxious about going in new directions, and a bit worried how things might turn out. In all our ways may we acknowledge you. We need you to make straight our paths, and to lead us in ways that neither damage one another, the environment or ourselves.

> Lord Jesus when we are hurting, we often lack confidence or motivation to try something different. It can seem so daunting. Please calm our fears, and may your Holy Spirit guide our feet and give us courage to explore, and to find new paths that lead to beautiful vistas, wonder and blessing, Amen.

Blog 85: Breathtaking Beauty in Unsettling Times

15th January 2022

A mandarin duck

There are so many choices to make every day. So often I want to make the safe choice, to do less, to hide. It seems so tempting. There are times when this is what we need to do, in order to heal.

But I also think there are times when God calls us to go out, to make that change, to speak when it is unpopular, to take that next step.

I am reminded of Jesus saying to Peter out on the boat, 'Come!' So Peter got out of the boat, and walked on water, and came to Jesus. 'But when he saw the wind, he was frightened, and he began to sink, and he cried out "Lord, save me". Immediately Jesus extended his hand to him and caught him.' (Matthew 14:29-31a)

It was night, and when Peter saw Jesus walk on water, he wanted to join him. When he was focused on Jesus he could do it, but when he doubted and got frightened he sank. Even then, Jesus caught him – immediately. What compassion and grace.

I had heard there were mandarin ducks in the area, and I thought I will never see any, it is not worth trying. Another part of me thought I will never know if I don't try. And so I went out, and found this beautiful bird on the river! When I found the motivation to try, I found the very thing I sought.

Now I am not saying that every time we try, we will find what we are looking for. But I am saying that if we don't try, we won't find it. So sometimes like Peter, we need to have the courage to try, and we might just find the very thing we seek.

> Gracious and patient God, you are so good to us, and you understand us when we feel negative and unmotivated, times when we give up trying. Lord Jesus, thank you that you speak to us and remind us what is to come, and that good things are still possible, even moments of breathing beauty and kindness. In unsettling days, may your Holy Spirit give us courage to get out of our boat, and to seek new adventures, and to continue to trust in your good purposes. In Jesus' name, Amen.

Blog 86: Eeyore Kind of Days

31st January 2022

A blue day!

Eeyore often seems to be feeling sad and gloomy – see the last page of the colour section. Even with his friends Winnie the Pooh, Tigger and Piglet, he can sound a bit mournful. And sometimes he just doesn't seem to know why, he just is.

I think we can all have Eeyore days, when we seem to get out of bed on the wrong side, and it doesn't matter how hard we try, we just can't shake that feeling of heaviness. These are days when we are low energy, often irritable, and completely resistant to anyone who has the audacity to try and cheer us up.

I guess, sometimes, we just need to give one another space to be sad. Sometimes there is a reason to be low mood – it could be an unpleasant conversation, a disappointment or a difficult anniversary. All these things could cause upset. At other times, there is no obvious reason – it is just a day we struggle.

I always remember the story of Job's comforters, who sat with him whilst he was questioning why so many bad things had happened to him. He lost his children, his home, his livelihood and his health. He lamented his plight, with tears and angst. His friends who sat by him, were a comfort, till they opened their mouth. They tried to provide answers, when there were none, and so they only made it worse. They even tried to suggest it might all have been Job's fault, and they increased his sense of distress.

When we are hurting, or just feeling a bit lost, we know that God is always willing to be with us. He never rejects us or belittles us. Rather In Isaiah 41:10, it says: 'Do not fear, for I am with you, do not be dismayed for I am your God, I will strengthen you and help you. I will uphold you with my righteous right hand.'

When we are having a difficult day, God tells us not to fear, for he is with us, and will strengthen us. When we are unsure, he will steady us, and help us. We have such a wonderful and faithful God!

> Gracious God, sometimes we have so many questions, we are in so much pain, that we can't begin to articulate what is wrong. We are just having a sad, kind of lonely day. Thank you Lord Jesus, that you are the one who stays with us in our distress, that you are closer than a brother. Your love lifts us up from the pit, and you encircle us with grace. Holy Spirit, thank you that when we have no answers we don't need to hide, that we can be honest, and that you give us people who will sit with us in companionable silence. Thank you for those people, Amen.

Blog 87: Living, not just Surviving

5th February 2021

Life in full colour!

(See the last page of the colour section)

It feels at the moment, that we are all just surviving, rather than living. The covid 19 virus has affected our lives in such a profound way, not just in terms of the number of people with long covid, or who have passed away. It has also meant that we have been isolated from one another, seeing our homes as safe, and going out as risky. Familiar patterns have become more time by ourselves, fewer outings, less socializing. It seems as if we are all in danger of becoming a recluse!

If we were trying to cram too much into life before the pandemic, a bit more space can be beneficial. However for many people it has meant that we feel cut off from the rest of the world. We are thankful to have food and a roof over our heads, but we are at risk from becoming more self orientated and less socially engaged.

Surviving can look different for different people. Maybe we are going to work, seeing family, and watching TV. Maybe we are waiting for an operation, and struggling with ill health. Or perhaps we are a bit disappointed with life, a bit low mood. It is as if we are living in black and white instead of colour.

When we are healing, whether from health issues, trauma or bereavement, surviving is sometimes all we can do, just getting through the day. Hopefully as the wound heals, and we get stronger, we can gradually begin to live, to find our identity, to dance, to dream. Let's not live life as second best, but appreciate every moment, to explore and be creative, to travel and to have adventures again.

In John 10:10 Jesus said, 'I have come that they (my sheep) may have life, life in all its fullness.'

We are reminded that God wants us to live full lives, lives of love, of learning, of prayer and compassion, and of sharing the richness of our faith with others. He still has a good purpose for us, even when for awhile, we cannot imagine what that could be. May we never give up hope, but be willing to go forward, at times maybe fearful or with reservations, but also with a sense of wonder and expectation.

> Gracious and generous God, you lavish your love on us, even when we are in dark places, just going through the motions in our lives, just surviving, because anything else is too hard. Lord Jesus, when we are ready, lift us out of that chasm, so our feet can be on the Rock, and that we can see the world in colour again. Holy Spirit, open our eyes to your beauty and goodness, and breathe your life into us afresh so we can live in your freedom, with hope and joy once more, Amen.

Section 3: SHARING OUR STORIES

My heart is stirred by a noble theme as I recite my verses for the king,
my tongue is the pen of a skillful writer

Psalm 45:1

The books the Holy Spirit is writing are living, and every soul a
volume in which the divine author makes a true revelation of his
word, explaining it to every heart, unfolding it in every moment.

Jean-Pierre de Caussade

The Bible makes it clear that every time that there is a story of faith,
it is completely original. God's creative genius is endless.

Eugene H. Peterson

Encourage one another, and build each other up, just as you are
doing.

1 Thessalonians 5: 11

One of the most wonderful gifts in the world is the experience of connection.
For us to know that we are not alone and forgotten is crucial for our sense of
well-being. I believe that we are all loved and valued by God, even if we are
unsure or have messed up. We are created to live in relationship with God
in Jesus Christ, knowing the cleansing, forgiveness and extravagant love of
God, that is offered freely to us. Living in relationship with God gives us our
grounding, our anchor, our sense of self.

Bruce Perry's book *Born for Love* is a beautiful book of people's
stories, and the love that can help people through the most difficult of
circumstances. The story of Trinity in chapter 7, reminds us that any
experiences of love, can help provide some-one with resilience and can
make all the difference to an outcome of a life. When someone has a
number of ACES (adverse childhood experiences), being noticed and
cared for by just one individual can be everything.

One of the ways that God can reveal himself is though our connection
with others. Being able to share, to trust, to value, to love is such a privilege.

175

It is not to be taken lightly, for in life we see so many misunderstandings, division and conflict. Being rejected can be so hurtful, and damaging.

However, God calls us to forgive and to build up communities of grace and connection, and it has been one of the privileges of this season, to have had contact with many individuals, and to hear more of your stories. I have been deeply moved and inspired by stories of adaptability and courage, of grace and faith. It has been inspirational to be able to share together on such a deep level.

I have been so encouraged by the prayers that have been said, the stories told, the tears shed, as well as the laughter and mirth of daily life! Often we seem to go through every emotion under the sun, repeatedly!

I asked a few people who have been part of this community of grace, if they would be willing to share something of their own stories, and to say a little about what has helped them through times of pain or adversity. We learn so much from one another, and find strength and wisdom in different voices. Longer term, I would love to form a wee community of people who would like to communicate and write, as I have met so many talented people along the way – poets, bloggers, creative writers, I would love to see everyone to write more, and to be read more also. Sadly there was not space in this particular place to hear every insight and inspiring story, but I would love to encourage more sharing in the future, if people are amenable!

I am grateful to my son Andrew for also wanting to participate in this. He has had a hard road to travel, and I am proud of him for wanting to use his experiences to encourage and support others.

For all those who have graciously agreed to write for this section of the book, thank you from the bottom of my heart. You are a wonderful community who seek to encourage others in times of pain and struggle with such beautiful sentiments and insights. You have blessed me, and I pray will bless many because of what you have written. Thank you for your courage, honesty and your generosity of spirit.

In the midst of many of these writings, there is a theme of the possibilities of transformations, and I wanted to finish this section with a quotation from John O'Donohue:

> From the black heart of winter, a miraculous, breathing plentitude
> of colour emerges. The beauty of nature insists on taking its time.

Everything is prepared. Nothing is rushed. The rhythm of emergence is a gradual slow beat always inching its way forward; change remains faithful to itself until the new unfolds in the full confidence of new arrival. Because nothing is script, the beginning of spring nearly always catches us unawares. It is there before we see it; and then we can look nowhere without seeing it.[11]

O'Donohue continues to speak of change as crossing new thresholds which emerge unsuspected as winter gives way to spring. This description of how transformation can take place gives us hope! It reminds us that on the surface things can seem the same for a very long time, and that we can feel frustrated as if we are just going through the motions. However God is at work and there is a healing in the depths of our being. One day we will recognise this change and welcome it for life will be less painful and less of a struggle.

The stories that follow are written by some of the people around me – they take different forms and give a variety of perspectives. I asked them to describe a struggle that they have had, or an issue that they have faced, and the resources that they have found that have helped them. My prayer is that though their stories, people will find something that they might relate to, and which may be an encouragement. They are stories about struggle, illness, disability, faith, identity and loss.

ANGUISH TO DESTINY by Muriel Stoddart

Anguish is one of those words you understand the meaning of by just the way it sounds. It has a gnarling rasp to it as you twist your mouth around it.[12]

The gnarling rasp of anguish became my constant companion in 2002, when I was overwhelmingly and suddenly diagnosed with lung disease. In a breath my identity and ability to function as a wife, mother, sister, friend was stolen by the diagnosis of Bronchiolitis Obliterans. My loudness, joy,

---

11 John O'Donohue, *Benedictus*, Bantam Press 2007, 64-5.
12 Ranata Suzuki in *A Life Half Lived* – https://ranata-suzuki.tumblr.com/post/177606458902/anguishits-one-of-those-words-you-understand.

love of singing and laughter was replaced by the very sound of anguish in my struggle to breathe – my 'suffocation' audible.

Rob Bell defines despair as 'the belief that tomorrow will be just like today.' My despair was in hospital admission after admission, battling for life, culminating in 2003 when The Freeman Hospital in Newcastle confirmed that without a lung transplant I was very life limited . . . a matter of months.

In the darkness I was being presented with grave clothes, and my very spirit groaned. In the groaning I could hear heaven sighing in love over me and in that sigh was comfort and peace. Jesus endured despair, and he knew and heard my groanings.

My groans were being translated into prayers, as Paul explains in Romans 8:26. The Holy Spirit takes hold of our human frailty to empower us in our weakness. At these times we don't even know how to pray, or know the best things to ask for, but the Holy Spirit rises up within us to super-intercede on our behalf, pleading to God with emotional sighs too deep for words. And I found that as I ascended in my own spirit my ears would pop.

Jesus' breath was my synchronisation with heaven. His breath was my life – on inhaling I would say internally JES and on exhaling US. Every breath a prayer.

I now know the monastics call this the breath prayer: JESUS.

I was moving from brooding with morbid thoughts to understanding Psalm 91:4,

> He will cover you with his feathers,
> He will shelter you with his wings.

That image refers to the wings of the cherubim resting on the mercy seat , a symbol of God's protection – and Jesus would years later refer to himself as a mother hen longing to shelter its chicks under its feathers.

The enemy – satan – tried to hold me in fear, hopelessness, despair, darkness but my spiritual vision was being developed, no matter how dark the hour. Black dark became the white light of resurrection as my identity was renewed in Christ.

How I clung onto, and still hold onto the tassels of Jesus' prayer shawl for healing.

I began to grasp how loved I was and not abandoned.

I came to a convergence point, knowing that everything I went through was propelling me to my ultimate destiny as a prayer intercessor. Intercession is a gift I began to exercise for others as others interceded for me.

> So now we draw near freely and boldly to where grace is enthroned, to receive mercy's kiss and discover the grace we urgently need to strengthen us in our time of weakness.
>
> Hebrews 4:16 TPT

I began to rest in his peace, intimacy, wisdom and strength.

In 2004 I asked to be removed from the active transplant list. I had moved from no man's land to being 'present'. What do I mean? I was once more present in family life, even though from a bed or wheelchair. Emotionally engaged. My quality of life had improved through natural and supernatural means.

Very graciously my team at The Freeman said the door was always open, as in truth all they saw before them was a compromised oxygen dependent patient relying on a cocktail of medications.

So we fast forward to 2022. I have sung with angels in worship. Worship changes the atmosphere and releases power.

Has anything changed in my lung function? No – which makes my life miraculous.

> We have a God who bends his ear to listen.
>
> Psalm 116:1-2 TPT

Here is how I pray the first 12 verses of this psalm, using that Bible version:

> I am passionately in love with God because he listens to me. He hears my prayers and answers them. As long as I live I'll keep praying to him, for he stoops down to listen to my heart's cry.
>
> Death once stared me in the face, and I was close to slipping into dark shadows. I was terrified and overcome with sorrow. I cried out to the Lord, 'God, come and save me!'
>
> He was so kind, so gracious to me. Because of his passion for me, he made everything right and he restored me. So I have learned from

my experience that God protects the vulnerable – for I was broken and brought low, but he answered me and came to my rescue.

Now I can say to myself and to all, 'Relax and rest, be confident and serene, for the Lord truly rewards those who simply trust him.' God has rescued my soul from death's fear, and dried my eyes of many tears. He has kept my feet firmly on his path, that I may please him and walk before Yahweh in the fields of life. Even when it seems I'm surrounded by many liars and my own fears, even though I am hurting in my suffering and trauma, I still stay faithful to God and speak words of faith.

So now, what can I ever give back to God to repay him for the blessings he has poured out on me?

Amen

What is your miracle?

Let it begin by saying out loud that Psalm 116 which I have been describing as my own experience. That is to meditate, to say it slowly and listen. To meditate in Hebrew means to SAY TO YOURSELF, not merely to 'think about'.

I pray you know the truth of God's light in your darkness because God's word IS light so every time you speak God's word you speak LIGHT into your heart. It is that SAME light that fills heaven . . .

Imagine . . . a God who bends his ear to listen. When you speak scripture out loud it moves from your mind to your heart as you say it. The word of God is alive (Hebrews 4:12).

Destiny . . . let Jesus be your journey, your road map, your guide . . . your final destination – not exhaustion, trauma, whatever that looks like for you. We are all walking each other home.

In case you want to make a sound track here are some of my favourites:
'Heroes' by Amanda Lindsay Cook
'Goodness of God', Jenn Johnson
'Take Courage' (radio version), Kristine Di Marco
'Overwhelming', Jeremy Riddle

I can be contacted at Muesto@virginmedia.com

CO-EXISTING WITH DYSLEXIA by Andrew Gardner

Please don't pick me. Please don't pick me. Please don't pick me . . .

I can feel the sweat on my hands. The teacher's eyes look around the classroom. I sit there saying to myself – please don't pick me, please don't pick me. Please don't pick me. Everyone is writing on the board – so uniform, so undeviating. The teacher's eyes land on me. I have to go up. I have to go up, but I do not want to. A hundred laps around the football pitch would be less daunting than this. I wipe the sweat of my hands on my trousers. I stand up and walk to the board. I grab the pen – it is slippy in my hands.

The question is so simple, the answer so easy – the communication so difficult. I begin to write. My 2 looks like an S. Is that a U or a V? Is it a minus sign or a slash? I've made it to the end. I take a step back, hands shaking. All the answers dance, but mine do not dance like the others. I return back to my chair. It will be ok I tell myself.

The teacher calls me back. 'It looks like a dog's breakfast.' The class sniggers. There is no escaping this moment, like many others. What a privilege it is to not be dyslexic.

Not all disabilities are visible, and so much trauma and discomfort could be avoided. The teacher had been informed that I was dyslexic, and yet here I am singled out with no justification. I felt mortified, embarrassed, humiliated, disillusioned.

Doing things that make me feel better doesn't solve the problem, and don't help in the long term. I am in the underworld with the other people trying to spell. I am trying to build a ladder to get to the sky city where people can spell. I am trying to get to the place where having dyslexia is not a barrier, not a limitation, not a hindrance.

I am at a point now where I am pretty close.

The things that help a little are typing on my own computer, which has become accustomed to my word pattern, and anticipates my path. Dyslexic friendly fonts help the letters to dance more uniformly.

I also usually choose to contribute verbally, and to write only when absolutely necessary and a computer is not available. I use strategies to help me cope. Playing computer games helped me to learn language, as well as just talking to people informally.

Who helped me most? People who listened to me as an individual, and worked together with me to find what was most supportive. Additional support needs teachers could be helpful when they advocated for me in the general school environment.

To anyone with dyslexia, or any other learning disability, remember: no one quite understands our world – not even fellow people understand how we exactly feel. There also isn't a solution to our problems. This can seem really daunting at times. If we keep trying we can get to a point where it is manageable and we can live being comfortable saying we have 'dyslexia' without feeling inferior.

Although one can never be free from dyslexia, we should keep fighting. It is the struggle itself that is most important, as we strive to be who we are. It doesn't matter that we will not beat it – the effort yields its own rewards.

Thinking out of the box, and having a visual three dimensional understanding, you can think in ways that others can't, and this can be a gift. As a mechanic, visual is what helps me to be an original problem solver.

DARKNESS NOT DARK IN CHRIST by Fergus Buchanan

This is the substance of a blog written in the Autumn of 2019 when I was undergoing chemotherapy for Multiple Myeloma, a blood cancer. The blogs came intermittently throughout my treatment and subsequent Stem Cell Transplant. They can be accessed at https://fcbuchanan.blogspot.com/

It's been a long haul and inevitable that I should be interested in the cancer stories of others. I have written about some of them in the past eight months. Obviously people of faith have featured most prominently but there have been others not believers but not to be ignored. Men and women who have coped with inspiring inner strength. The best of those stories are those in which you connect with a 'voice', a sense of the person behind the words, a person willing to be honest, open and vulnerable. The very best are those in which the person shares things they have learned about themselves and about God even while acknowledging the pain, disorientation, weakness and despair.

What have I learned about myself? Well, that might be the subject of future blogs. Maybe. What is most important is what I am learning about God. Even as I write this I want to correct that. Really it's what I am *experiencing* about God that is most important. I've always *known* about God. It was in my head. And it would be wrong to say that I have never had profound experiences of God and the love he has shown for humankind in Jesus. It's just that some things I feel I have discovered about God on a personal level in the past I have been reluctant to share and to preach. And these things have become more important, no vital to me in these cancer days. Yes I have sometimes preached and written about 'the dark side of God', his judgement, his mysterious providence, his discipline. But when you get down to it, I have been nervous, reluctant to go there.

So unlike Paul, who in the face of breath-taking revelations from the eternal world wrote:

> To keep me from becoming conceited, I was given a thorn in my flesh, a messenger of Satan, to torment me. Three times I pleaded with the Lord to take it away from me. But he said to me, 'My grace is sufficient for you, for my power is made perfect in weakness.' Therefore I will boast all the more gladly about my weaknesses, so that Christ's power may rest on me. That is why, for Christ's sake, I delight in weaknesses, in insults, in hardships, in persecutions, in difficulties. For when I am weak, then I am strong.
>
> 2 Corinthians 12:7-10

So unlike Peter, who writes of all the blessings we receive in the life, death and resurrection of Jesus:

> In all this you greatly rejoice, though now for a little while you may have had to suffer grief in all kinds of trials. These have come so that the proven genuineness of your faith – of greater worth than gold, which perishes even though refined by fire – may result in praise, glory and honor when Jesus Christ is revealed.
>
> 1 Peter 1:6-7

So unlike the unknown writer of the letter to the Hebrews, who without a tremor of apology writes:

> Endure hardship as discipline; God is treating you as his children. For what children are not disciplined by their father? . . . We have all had human fathers who disciplined us and we respected them for it. How much more should we submit to the Father of spirits and live! They disciplined us for a little while as they thought best; but God disciplines us for our good, in order that we may share in his holiness. No discipline seems pleasant at the time, but painful. Later on, however, it produces a harvest of righteousness and peace for those who have been trained by it. Therefore, strengthen your feeble arms and weak knees. 'Make level paths for your feet,' so that the lame may not be disabled, but rather healed.

Hebrews 12:7-13

So unlike Jesus, who knew that heavy almost soul-destroying darkness in Gethsemene such that his whole constitution – body, mind and spirit – threatened to come apart completely. And yet Luke tells us that an angel was sent, an emissary from the eternal world, to strengthen him, to assure him that the 'cup' was worth the tasting for herein lay the salvation of the whole universe. Who sent the angel? His heavenly Father, who loved him. It's what the Psalmist says:

> If I say, 'Surely the darkness will hide me and the light become night around me,' even the darkness is not dark to you; the night will shine like the day, for darkness is as light to you.

Psalm 139:11-12

It may not be a perfect application for a man with cancer but it's a truth that needs to be grasped. The Psalmist is celebrating the eternal presence of God in every circumstance. The darkness is not dark to him. He is present in the darkness working out his perfect and loving will.

Even Gethsemane did not see the end of testing for Jesus. Many have been the attempts to soften the moment of Jesus' dereliction, his anguish at the abandonment of God while he died on the cross. He had read the Psalm. He had probably memorised it as a boy in the synagogue. He had even inspired it from all eternity as the second person of the Trinity. But now he experienced it, as one us, God in the flesh, and so he cries out the most gut-wrenching words in the whole of human history: 'My God, my God, why have you forsaken me?' (Psalm 22: 1)

In a preaching I heard from Prof. Donald Macleod he once referred to the humanity of Jesus and how he identified with us completely even to the extent of knowing the loss of God. 'Tis mystery all! The immortal dies,' wrote Wesley in one of the greatest of all hymns. Stuart Townend invites us to sing:

> How deep the Father's love for us,
> How vast beyond all measure,
> That he should give his only Son
> To make a wretch his treasure.
> How great the pain of searing loss –
> The Father turns his face away,
> As wounds which mar the Chosen One
> Bring many sons to glory.

The most dramatic line in this verse speaks of the agony of the Father turning his face away from his beloved Son on the cross. God must have known of this moment from all eternity, the moment of redemption for the whole universe, the moment of redemption for me, through the suffering of the Son he loved.

Those with bad memories of childhood may be sensitive to a line like this, as there are human fathers who turn away from their children, and worse. But remember, 'God was in Christ redeeming the world to himself'. Townend's line is trying to express the awful mystery that on the cross, God was taking the terrible break that sin makes into himself, in order that all things should be mended, healed, sorted for ever.

Father, take away my nervous reluctance to go there. You not only saw it, you willed it for the humanity you loved. A more courageous man than I, the apostle John, said:

> God loved the world so much that he gave his one and only Son so that whoever believes in him should not perish but have eternal life.

> John 3:16

Paul writes:

> He who did not spare his own Son, but gave him up for us all—how will he not also, along with him, graciously give us all things? . . . For I am convinced that neither death nor life, neither angels nor

demons, neither the present nor the future, nor any powers, neither height nor depth, nor anything else in all creation, will be able to separate us from the love of God that is in Christ Jesus our Lord.

Romans 8: 32-39

Out of his love for us he did not spare his Son. What sustains me at present is the assurance that God has loved me so much that he did not spare his only Son to deal with the darkness of sin that separates me from him and assures me of a place in his eternal Kingdom. So whatever darkness falls has not pushed God out or his love. The darkness is not dark to him. The light of his loving purpose is at the core moving my life according to his pace towards the completion.

I don't know 'the reasons why'. Neither did that man I dare to call my brother, the Apostle Paul. He looked forward to the Day when all that was unclear would be made clear. It's there in 1 Corinthians 13. Read it. And not just the bit they read at weddings.

> Now we see but a poor reflection in a mirror; then we shall see face to face. Now I know in part; then I shall know fully, even as I am fully known. (verse 12)

I'm amazed that I've written so much recently and not mentioned Ron Dunn, an American pastor, who experienced much darkness in his life but was a powerful witness for his God revealed in Jesus. In his book *When Heaven Is Silent* he speaks about living with the question 'why?' He says something quite astonishing. With all he has gone through and it is more than most of us will ever be called upon to endure he believes that at the end of all things when he comes into God's presence in all the wonder and the glory the questions will not matter. I'm with him.

The question for me – and patient reader for you too – is for this moment. How deeply do we really know this God revealed through Jesus? Oh and there is another question, how far do we trust him? This God whose darkness is not dark, whose love will never efface us from his heart, whose love will never decay, whose good purpose is moving on through the worst. Ron wrote:

> I confess I'm still trying to get an answer to my 'why?' And I'm still getting the silent treatment. But it's all right. I trust him.

I'm with Ron.

DARKNESS to LIGHT by Lynsey Brennan

I must strive, I must strive
I must strive, to stay alive

Keep going, keep going, I say
I'm moving fast, but don't know the way

I starve, I date, I study, I mate

This void's an abyss, what is it I miss?
Why are we here, what is it I fear?

I work hard, I work late
Play roulette with my fate

Sex, lies, pain, hurt
I don't want to move forward

The voices, the fears, the noise in my head
Why can't I die on my cancer bed?

Crash, burn, fall, it's dark
Is this the end?

A letter, a card, a gift, a call
Humanity's best, a touch more than the rest

Why does she care? What is her goal?
She cares deeply for me, a lost, broken soul

'You're fearfully and wonderfully made', I'm told
A sweet, precious child, that He wants to hold

Who? Me? Are you sure?
My life is dark, my life is pain

The deceit, the abuse, the neglect
Have all left their mark

I'm thin, I'm broken, a new life growing taken
But you tell me, through Jesus, not all is forsaken

For he is the way, the truth and the life
The great 'I am', the healing Lamb

So, I walk from the darkness into the light
Trusting this saviour, no judgement, no fight

I worship, I pray, I seek and I find

A love everlasting, a love like no other
No longer alone, I'm a sister, a brother

I've a family of love and peace from above

I walked through the valley of the shadow of death
But it didn't consume me, Christ's light set me free

Come to me all who are weary and burdened,
And I will give you rest

I no longer strive, I'm truly alive.

The author writes:

Faith in Jesus was like a light finally being put on in my life. Everything looked different and I suddenly had a higher, more in-depth appreciation of all things. My relationships and friendships with others were strengthened and I now notice, enjoy and celebrate life's everyday blessings, however small.

In the 14 years since I've become a follower of Jesus, I've faced many more trials in my life, but my faith has given me an inner resilience, and a deep hope that I need to keep moving forward. As the Christian song goes, 'I am no longer a slave to fear, I am a child of God.'

Eternal hope flows through me, and now I'm driven to love others who are experiencing their own darkness, and who could be made whole by a relationship with their living God. I serve now as a minister within the Church of Scotland.

Revd Lynsey Brennan can be contacted at:
lbrennan@churchofscotland.org.uk

GREY by Lesli Lawrie

I gave you all the colours you needed.
And day after day you mixed up grey*

Fizzing, foaming grey cocktail of being misunderstood
Assaulted identity
Teeth vibrating
Fists clenched impotently

Steely grey spring of rejection
Coiled, ready to react
An innocent comment
Two-way regret

Tangled grey spaghetti of confusion
Winding relentlessly
Facts and reason evasive
Too slippery for the brain to hold

Leaden grey knot of anxiety
Greets inevitably each morning
Insurmountable obstacles
Take up residence in the abdomen

Severed, frayed grey fronds of bereavement
Quivering, desperately reaching
For what is no longer there
Raw nerves. Searing agony

Vast grey mountainous landscape of loneliness
A single set of footprints
Photographs of never-to-be-shared memories
Slipping through sad fingers

Bulky grey burden of responsibility
Advice disregarded
Heated exchanges
Shoulders weary as the buck stops here

Rising grey rungs of expectation
Another and another and another
Never ending ladder
Foot follows foot follows foot

Soft grey enveloping mist of depression
Numbing pain
Seductively whispering
Detach, sink, float, cease . . .

Sinister grey shadows of fear
Suggestive, paralysing
Breath-robbing thieves
Arrest the lungs

Chilling greyness of terminal illness
Tingeing the skin as well as the soul
Hopelessness creeps
Eyes weep

Silver grey droplets
Rain, tears
Cathartic rivulets flow at last
Toxins released from the heart

Listen . . .
Look . . .
For where there is sorrow there is also joy

Laser sharp accuracy
Softer than a whisper
The Light of Love himself
Comes
Perspex-tive**

Bring me your greys
Let my Love shine through them
All the colours you need
A hope-filled , healing rainbow
My promise. My bow.

Notes

* I learned to mix colours when I was 23. Until then, the advice from playgroup, school, brownies and high school art had been, 'Don't mix the colours.'

When at last I had the privilege of my own class I determined to only provide the primary colours red, blue and yellow as well as white (and small amounts of black on demand) to give the children every opportunity to mix up the exact hue they needed, as well as enjoy the wonder of it all.

They started school in August. The paints were available all day, every day. And every day at 3 o clock, the pallets were filled with grey paint. I was so disappointed.

Then I believe God said, 'This is how I feel about my children.' And the poem began to form.

** In high school I learned for the first time that by shining a beam of light through a block of uninteresting-looking perspex, you could see the full spectrum of rainbow colours. The play on words perspex/ perspective makes me smile.

Postscript

I attended a wet-felt workshop a few months ago. It was part of a range of craft opportunities provided by Ellel Grange on their 'Healing Through Creativity' weekends.

I was surrounded by the most beautiful deep colours of softest lambswool, but I knew what I needed to do. Using the darker shades mixed with grey I created a visual representation of most of the above verses, laying all my greyness down before my Father God. The workshop leader looked a little perplexed at the gloomy piece I was creating when so much vibrancy and joy was happening in the other pieces being created around me but she was respectful and once I had finished asked me to go and fill a bowl with water for the next part of the process.

When I returned, a white cloth had been placed over my work, ready for the next step. It looked like a shroud.

Clean water, olive oil soap, massaged, hard pressed, squeezed, rinsed, thrown on the floor to shock the wool into bonding, held up to the light. The symbolism is all there in the process.

She said 'That's a lovely piece of felt.'

I finally understood the line from the old hymn 'death of death and hell's destruction.' Death's agents and all their hold on us has ended. The grey times happen but they need not define us. At the cross, Jesus took it all on himself, and he offers freedom, colour, light and life to all who want to find it.

Afterword

Six months on and the P1 children are now mixing colours! The painting area is always busy and the walls are covered in vibrant paintings of every hue.

LIFE CAN ONLY BE UNDERSTOOD BACKWARDS by Linda

Life can only be understood backwards. The trouble is it must be lived forwards. Forwards is fine, providing we daily trust in a good and sovereign God.

> For now we see only a reflection as in a mirror; then we shall see face to face. Now I know in part; then I shall know fully, even as I am fully known.   (1 Corinthians 13:12)

> Taste and see that the LORD is good; blessed is the one who takes refuge in him. (Psalm 34:8)

> Go in peace. The journey on which you go is under the eye of the LORD. (Judges 18:6)

I am surprised to realise that I have reached an age where some hindsight is possible! As I reflect on some of the situations that have been a part of my life's story, I am ever grateful for the people who have walked the road with me. Some have walked with me all my life. Others have walked for a specific time in my life; all have added something special to my life. I am also very grateful to the people who have supported me in my faith journey which started at a very young age. Hindsight allows me to understand the significance of these things: faith, family, friends.

However, when we are living life in the present as we must do, hindsight is not an option. There have been times when I have wanted answers to the 'why' questions. Why did that baby die when so much was resting on her as the way to a new beginning? Why did that toddler die when he had such a healing influence on a broken-hearted family? Why did that sister-in-law die without warning in her forties? These are just a few of the situations where knowing only part of the story was difficult to accept in the moment. I did not want that reflection in a mirror: I wanted the face-to-face opportunity to ask about the future. It was pointed out to me that God's timing is perfect but that seemed a hard thing to accept at the time. I was extremely grateful to friends who were willing to accept my sadness and play a part in the healing process but I found it hard to see only in part.

The kindness of one person played a huge part in our family life. This person offered our family her home on the beautiful Isle of Arran as she felt we needed a holiday. We accepted this kind offer with gratitude, believing it to be a one-off gesture. Twenty years later we were still going on holiday to Arran to the same house. These holidays had a huge effect on our family and shaped our family life in ways we could never have imagined. The house and the island became our refuge for many years as we tasted the goodness and the refuge of God through this lady. Although we faced some challenging times, we also had many good things happen as I learned to be content with God's timing and plans but I confess to being a slow learner.

The loss of a much-loved person and a person's response to it is so very personal. As I spend time with my grandchildren, I would like to think that we are making good memories together. This is important to me as I realise that, for me, having good memories of a person has allowed me to laugh, smile, cry and crucially live with few regrets. When my own parents died within a few months of each other I was very sad. Seventeen years on I still think of them every day with gratitude and often a laugh. They were older when they died and had lived a full life. I could appreciate that, their deaths were 'in season.' The memories I have is a legacy beyond compare. I believe this is why the 'get together' after a funeral is important. It is a time to share memories and speak of the person. I hope my grandchildren have a real hoolie at my funeral and humour is the order of the day. My heart goes out to those who were unable to have such times during the recent covid pandemic.

My faith is very important to me but it does not make me immune to the hard life knocks. Hindsight allows me to know that it has been my refuge even if I am too stubborn to always acknowledge it. Family and friends also play a huge part in any grieving process. In the days when autograph books were in vogue my Granny wrote in mine, 'Make new friends but keep the old, for one is silver the other gold.' What a wonderful piece of advice for a young child. Spending time in relationships is worth every minute. We are made to be in community and friends form a large part of our community. Recently when a granddaughter was diagnosed with cancer, I was amazed at the support given by friends old and new. What a blessing it was to know folks cared in so many different ways: a card, two freshly baked scones on the doorstep, a bag of sweets, a bouquet of flowers, a candle, a donation to teen cancer, prayer and so so much more.

Oh, if truth be told there was still an element of the old 'why this beloved child Lord?' The doctor told my son that this would be a hard and long journey for my granddaughter. It was helpful to be reminded that the journey on which we were going was under the eye of the Lord. I still experienced some anxious times but once again these were underpinned by faith, family and friends.

LOSING MUM by Evelyn Wright

Although mum spent two days in hospital in a coma before she died, I still felt shock at the unexpected stroke that put her there. Despite being told by the medical staff that it would only be a matter of time, I clung to the hope that maybe this was a mistake and that she would wake up. It was no mistake as I found out, as she breathed her last breath with me by her side. I was glad that I was there, but I felt for my sister who hadn't made it back to the hospital on time and was clearly devastated at not being there.

While the funeral was a sad occasion there were moments of joy with one of mum's many poems being read out which was as follows.

Behind the scenes

It's the little things that mean the most
It's the little things that count
It's not the ones who shout and boast
Or the ones who flaunt and flount

It's the quiet ones behind the scenes
With their countless deeds untold,
Who reap rewards and riches
As their thoughtful lives unfold.

They maybe don't get many thanks
As they quietly work away
But in their heart they are content
As they come to the end of the day.

To make other people happy
Is what they aim to do,
And have no time to spare for themselves
They're too busy with me and you.

At the end of the funeral my mum's coffin was carried out to the beautiful sound of her piano playing which had been recorded a few years beforehand. She would have loved that scenario.

With all the busyness of organising everything I really hadn't had the time to have a good cry, and even at the funeral I was making sure everything was running smoothly, however a few weeks later I was alone in my mum's house. I had stayed overnight and my siblings were coming over later that day so we could sort through my mum's belongings. I was sitting in my mum's chair, with my breakfast on the lap tray and I had UCB radio playing in the background. A song by Ryan Stevenson came on, I had never heard it before but the chorus said it all and as I listened to it I cried and cried and cried. It was such a release and even two years after my mum's death I still cry when I hear that song and it continues to be a great source of comfort.

The chorus of the song is:

> It's okay to cry,
> It's okay to fall apart
> You don't have to try to be strong when you are not
> And it may take some time
> To make sense of all your thoughts,
> But don't ever fight your tears
> 'Cause there is freedom in every drop.
> Sometimes the only way to heal a broken heart
> Is when we fall apart.

Mum's greatest wish was that her children all kept in touch with each other which we have been doing with phone calls, text messages and where possible meeting up. Also in mum's honour and memory we are having a belated (due to covid restrictions) 90th birthday meal, with her children and their children all meeting together. Mum dearly wanted to survive until she was 90 and to have a family party for her 90th. We're so sorry that mum won't be there but we intend to do her proud.

For those who are struggling I would say don't ever give up hope of feeling better, cry when they need to and don't be hard on themself. Writing about feelings in a journal can be cathartic. Supportive family and friends would be great to have around but I realise not always possible. Always be kind to yourself and do one kind thing for yourself every day.

evelynwright2610@gmail.com

STORIES OF STRENGTH by Laura Miller

In the bleak midwinter of January 2009, my husband I were married on a rare day of crisp blue skies and dazzling sunshine. James and I had met at at a time when my health was stable enough to allow part time work and romantic pursuits. A time of joyful restoration; of our heart's desires coming to fruition, as we planned our future together.

Several decades of complex ill health meant my levels of mobility constantly waxed and waned. I'd had times of being housebound before. So we both knew to continue to expect my illnesses to affect daily life.

My ability to work hit rapid decline as old symptoms reared their head and I lost my job. Severe allergic reactions attacked my already compromised immune system, and my ability to stand began to crumble as my body grew weaker. I could only walk to the nearest lamp post to our flat, and back again. This distance declined, no matter how much effort I forced into my steps. Although I'd had my mobility affected like this before, my instincts were that something more permanent was afoot. I sensed long term loss of the strength in my legs. Exercise was not stopping this onslaught against my health. I was no stranger to obtaining mobility by other means, so I began to ask for help.

One day two physios came to visit with a rollator to try and give me something to hold onto as I walked. But I collapsed after a few steps, injuring myself. The world I'd fought so hard to remain part of was rapidly retreating. I was too unsafe on my feet to make it past our front door. In less than a year I went from employable to jobless and from having moderate mobility to being housebound again.

The flat we lived in had a shared entrance with around fifteen steps to the pathway. I now needed a wheelchair to get around outside. I'd had my own chair in the past, so mentally this was not the worst adjustment. It was the reality that this small flight of steps was now my obstacle to freedom that brought me to despair.

We began the task of applying to have a ramp fitted. There were similar properties in the area where the same number of steps were now an easy to access slope. All of these properties were managed by a housing association, meaning not only did we need evidence of my needs to set the application process in motion, but there would be other legalities to battle after that.

At a time when we should have been enjoying the honeymoon after glow together, we were instead wrestling to keep me from being imprisoned in our own home.

Bureaucracy has its own ability to lock down or open up opportunities in life. From the medical professionals who refused to give us concrete evidence I needed to back up my need for a ramp, to the Social Work departments that were equally unsupportive; I now had both a short flight of stairs and a tangle of red tape keeping me inside.

My husband was bearing the burden of knowing when he was at work, I would be stuck by myself inside our home. His dual role of being both a provider and carer had become a guilt-ridden balancing act. He too was being imprisoned by the unwillingness of others to act. It felt cruel.

Every fruitless battle brought us to tears.

My life was being shrunk by forces beyond my control. I emailed any politician I could find. I told my story to a newspaper. The emails bore no fruit. The newspaper did not print my story.

Cabin fever strikes faster than most folk imagine. First, there are the same walls in the same rooms that make up the boundaries of your life. Then, there is the necessity to negotiate every interaction with a world outside those walls. A world that was only accessible via could support my shaking body down the offending steps and into my manual chair. We needed me to have my own electric wheelchair and a ramp to get me independent again.

I missed opportunities to see friends for coffee or have fresh air and a change of scenery. Worst of all, it led to not attending my GP regularly and missing opportunities to get help with the rest of my health. A random blood test revealed I was severely deficient in vitamin D. This likely occurred long before my decline in mobility, but no real access to sunshine meant having to rely on supplements alone.

Knowing that the flick of a pen, a tick in a box could have allowed us to pursue my freedom was just as immobilising as having no stability in my legs.

I was grieving constantly. More than that; the reality that the systems we relied on were refusing to rescue me, were completely destroying my confidence. In the past I would have taken this time of loneliness to reflect on my failure to overcome it. Thankfully at this point in my life I knew I was not at fault, and that there others suffering similar circumstances .

Countless people with disabilities in the Western World are at the mercy of being disbelieved or having their needs dismissed. The dawning realisation that fighting for basic adaptations is now their ongoing reality can be truly shocking. It's not the way they thought civilised societies worked. The resulting damage can eat at the core of who they believe themselves to be. Progress involves adapting to this new normal; one where negotiating support is now ever present. Progress that takes courage and resilience; but which can be hindered in a blink.

I plugged into podcasts online that told me similar stories to my own. When the boiling pot of frustration threatened to engulf me, I knew my struggle was wrapped up in a bigger picture. A telephone counselling service run by disabled people for disabled people became a lifeline. Mostly they listened. I hated hearing my voice tell the same story over and over. The fears that I sounded negative, or just plain boring, were kept at bay.

I know now that small seeds of wisdom were sewn by the counsellor who listened. She shared little snippets of her own life. Seeds of comfort. A taste of coming to terms with the loss of control, and a reassurance that this time was not just a waste of my potential.

I continued my studies with the Open University; a creative writing module that stretched my skills. Friends organised times of fellowship where they would visit and I would host. Rebellious times of enjoying our home, reminding me of the safety of it's walls. When it is other people causing part of our pain; we need our friends to remind us not all the world is against us.

It would be over a year until living in limbo stopped. We had to sell our flat and buy another in a new area to find freedom. The new flat also had stairs from the door to the path. But this time when we asked for a ramp, the powers that be said yes. They said yes instantly. It was as simple and as complex as that. Strong, burly men with grim faces and sparkling welding torches deftly melted metal parts to metal other parts. I watched my ramp come together in a noisy ballet of good engineering and hot flames.

New lessons now. A crash course via learning it the hard way alone on how to choose and buy an electric wheelchair. Buying a new flat had lost us money. The sweetener in this exchange was the gaining of gardens to our property, front and back.

It was not an overnight success, but this the part of the journey meant I was no longer at the total mercy of folk saying no. James regained a wife no longer trapped by concrete walls.

The transition to using my new ramp and my new chair came with fresh challenges. A small wheel on the back of the chair snapped off in the first week, meaning I was at risk of toppling. A stranger leapt across a busy main road to assist me, seeing my distress. There were huge hyper-ventilated gasps of fear that day. Nowadays, I am on my third electric chair. Powered by gigantic batteries that hold me stable to the ground as I travel.

Seeking counselling on the phone had paved the way to realising there would always be someone who could empathise. This in turn has led to me continue to develop friendships with other people who need the same kind of support. Many of these friendships have blossomed online. The memories of being housebound are now softened by the ability it gave me to reach out to others.

Loneliness can test our hearts and minds hard. There is always a way to form bonds with others who will understand our hurts and frustrations. Reaching out was my lifeline, helping me remember the strength there is in friends and fellowship.

SUBMISSION by Margaret Whyte

When I began to write this, to save my work I entitled the file 'Submission'; meaning something I was going to submit. I hadn't actually thought much about that word before. It can be a document given as I had meant but it does have a more sinister connotation, the act of allowing someone or something to have power over you.

My younger sister, brother and I didn't have the best of parents: our father was a hard abusive man and our mother a friendly feckless soul who adored him and would never have challenged him: submission was an earliest lesson.

It is a desperate thing that events of one's early life haunt one forever and frequently. My choice was to submit to these hurtful thoughts or to rise above them and overcome. There are various mechanisms which have helped me.

I truly think that it is love which has saved me. The love of God in Christ Jesus but God also gave me a beautiful loving Christian grandmother. For various reasons I've never quite understood, as a small child she frequently took me away from all that was corrosive at home, though I've had to deal with the fact that I escaped, unlike Robert and Christine. There were day trips with various groups of very large bosomed, impressive women and the wonderful caring minister of the Baptist Church. I was lucky, blessed. Her love has made me, and saved me. I knew she loved me more than her own life.

She was the church officer in the Baptist Church across the busy Paisley Road in Renfrew. Traffic stopped when crippled by arthritis she hobbled with her zimmer to her Church twice a day, a great Christian witness;

everyone knew her. She spent most of her time there and my happiest times were there helping her do the cleaning. She sat on a chair while mopping floors with the most foul smelling, though effective concoction. She played piano and organ by ear, a great gift and had a lovely alto voice. We filled the church with our voices and our hearts with the beautiful inspiring hymns she played.

Her love for others, for God, for her church, her generosity when she had so little, her lack of prejudice, except against the Church of Scotland minister who passed her window every day smoking a pipe, all these things I learned from her.

This is my salvation. Humble service, love, joyful submission.

But also having a less than easy father role model, I found salvation, joy and release in the love I knew was mine from my heavenly Father. I know it doesn't work for everyone, but knowing I did have a Father who loved me unconditionally was my salvation.

I didn't have a conversion experience which was necessary in Baptist circles, but I was also very aware that God walked or carried me through my life. I have always walked with God beside me. In 1968 aged 17 I felt called by God into service. I thought he wanted me to be a missionary in Outer Mongolia, the only outlet of service for women.

Coincidentally that was also the year I met Tom, the man who would become my husband, whom I have known and loved and been loved by for 53 years. Love and loving, giving and receiving, submission and partnering . . . that is my salvation. Called into service? This went right out the window. It was either him or the Church . . . I chose him.

Coincidentally it was also the year the General Assembly of the Church of Scotland decided women could be ordained as ministers of Word and Sacrament.

Ordained myself in 1988: humble service, loving people, which is not always easy, challenging fascinating situations, the joy of preaching the Gospel, touching others with God's love and grace, working with wonderful children in church and schools, has been my salvation. A small mousey person who wouldn't have said boo to anything, who in fact tried from a young age to be invisible, was turned into something God could channel and use. God knew the gifts he had given and which were lost somewhere deep within me, waiting to be unearthed.

Salvation is also in beauty. Despite the world being a terrible place at times, there is also immense beauty. I am able to immerse myself in that beauty and always seek that 'which is good and true and lovely' etc. I try very hard to remember what St Paul says and not dwell on darkness and badness.

I love the fecundity and awe inspiring beauty of nature. Growing things in my garden, I

My grandmother is on the left behind me.

can grow away from corrosive thoughts and blossom; weeding, I weed out sadness and isolation. God is right beside me. Look into the face of a rose and you really do look into the face of God.

In Art and Architecture I feel the goodness and greatness of the God given gifts to mankind. Raphael's 'Sistine Madonna and Child,' Michelangelo's Sistine Chapel, Moses and David, the solid majestic wonder of my city Glasgow; the techno-wizardry and inventiveness of human kind helps me override all the bad. I thrill every time I see an aeroplane ascend, my spirit ascends. Driving along the motorway I see not traffic at an annoying standstill but the ingenuity and teeming heartbeat of women and men.

Lastly, I have found Neuro-Linguistic Programming, NLP for short, very helpful. Tom introduced me to that and its various elements. For example when a difficult memory wells up, my father becomes the Wizard, in the Wizard of Oz. I can put things in little boxes and file them away. They do rise up again to bite me from time to time but get consigned once again. I will not submit to the darkness but will live in the light that is Christ my Saviour who found me and who did and has always carried me to my home in him. Praise be to God.

THE BLESSINGS OF GRIEF by David J. McLachlan

At first glance, the above title may seem a strange one. However, I chose it deliberately because it reflects my own experience, and in this short piece, I will try to explain why I think grief can bring many blessings – often unexpected ones.

In particular, I want to focus on my two closest, and most recent, times of grief (I suspect that grief will be part of my life until I shake off this mortal coil!). Our son, Iain, passed away 8 years ago. He was 35 years of age and had cancer. My wife, Rita, passed to her rest 2 years ago. She had a number of health conditions, and, thankfully, covid was not one of them.

In Iain's case, we had a few months' notice that his condition was terminal, and consequently had some time to prepare ourselves for his passing. That is not to say that, when it came, it made his death any easier to bear. It didn't, but the help and support my wife and I received during those months were undoubtedly blessings, and ones I hold dear to this day.

There was of course the help we got from our GP surgery, not least the District Nurses who visited the house to deal with his meds and personal care. When they were around, there was much laughter (Iain had a great sense of humour). They also supported Rita and me, and answered any questions or concerns we had.

We also received support and help from the Prince & Princess of Wales Hospice in Glasgow, mostly through personal contact with their specialist nurse, Ann, who could not have been more supportive, especially at the end. At his own request, Iain died at home, but Ann assured us that, if needed, a Hospice bed would be available.

Ann, together with two of the District Nurses who had cared for Iain, came to his funeral, and that meant so much to Rita and me.

They kept in touch with us for a time afterwards, and we both were appreciative of that. Moreover, the Hospice offered Bereavement Counselling, and other support, and although Rita decided it wasn't for her – a decision she later said she regretted – I accepted the offer, and found it very helpful and cathartic. Claire, my counsellor, seemed to have endless patience as she listened to my ramblings, and I will always be in her debt.

Whilst mentioning the Hospice, I must also include Marie Curie Cancer Care nurses, who came as often as staffing allowed to stay and watch over Iain overnight for the last month or so of his life. Their help and support were invaluable, and meant that Rita and I managed to get some sleep.

Support and practical help also came from family, friends, neighbours, and many in our Church family. From sending cards and letters (we received over 80) to telephone calls and both Rita's and my sisters coming to make our meals and look after us during the day so that we could be at Iain's bedside in his final days, and the many people who turned up for his funeral on a cold December afternoon, we felt supported, cared for, and blessed.

Iain's friends were a Godsend too. They made sure that he was included as much as possible in what they did during his last months, and I know he appreciated that. His Christian faith was important to him, as indeed it was to us, and his friends from the Church kept in touch with him to the end.

As the months went on, family, friends, neighbours, and Church family continued to look out for us, so we continued to feel supported, cared for, and, yes, blessed.

One other blessing which I have not mentioned so far is that of the many memories we have of Iain. From his birth, growing up via school, Sunday School, the Boys' Brigade (in which he later was to become a leader/helper) to his becoming an adult. Happy memories: times when laughter was heard all through the house; memories captured in the many photographs taken over the years. To my mind, the memories are the biggest blessings of all. There isn't a day passes that I don't recall something Iain said or did or that we experienced together.

As I indicated earlier, my most recent grief experience came with Rita's passing two years ago. Unlike Iain's death, Rita's was not expected, at least not when it came. She was in hospital, and had seemed to be getting better, and I was told by the doctor who was treating her that if she continued to make the progress she had been making, she could be home by the end of that week (we were speaking on the Tuesday).

On the Thursday of the same week I received a telephone call from the hospital advising me to go to the ward because Rita's condition had deteriorated rapidly. I did so, and was able to spend the last hour or so of her life at her bedside, holding her hand.

Of course it was hard and, yes, I cried. The woman I had known for over 49 years, and had been married to for over 44, had just died. Yet I still regard my being able to be with her for that last hour was a blessing in my grief. My reason for saying that is that I got an opportunity that few others had at that time. We still had covid restrictions at the time, and so many people were unable to be with their dying loved ones, a fact which has been well documented in the news and elsewhere. I was able to be at Rita's side when she breathed her last – a blessing which I will always treasure.

Another blessing from both Iain's and Rita's passing is that their suffering came to an end. No more would Iain require morphine to deal with the pain caused by the cancer. For Rita too the suffering was over. She did not have covid, but she had other health conditions, some which she had for most of her life. She had also been diagnosed with Parkinson's Disease, and that had severely affected her mobility, which frustrated her more and more as the days went on. It is indeed a blessing to know that her suffering and Iain's were over.

Once again the support network got to work, and I needed it every bit as much as – possibly even more than – I did when Iain died, and I was blessed as a result of it. If I am honest, I think I still need it. I am therefore so grateful for a neighbour who occasionally hands in some home made soup (mine always tastes rotten!), for family, friends and neighbours who call me or contact me on social media to make sure I am all right and for anyone who asks how I am doing, and takes the time to listen to my reply.

I am still grieving the loss of my darling wife. We were married for over 44 years, and they brought so many happy memories which are mine to keep for ever. I miss her terribly, but I can hear her voice quite clearly telling me to get on with things, and that I do not need to worry about her now.

That brings me to the biggest blessing of all. I said earlier that Rita, Iain, and I were/are Christians. That means that I firmly believe that death is not the end for any of us. There is a life to come; a life where there is no suffering, or tears, or any of the injustices we have in this world.

That is where, I am confident, Rita and Iain are now. No blessing can possibly be bigger or more important than that.

david.maclachlan53@hotmail.co.uk

Section 4: HIDING, HEALING, HOPE – SOME RESOURCES

Fear not, for I am with you, be not dismayed, for I am your God. I will strengthen you, I will help you. I will uphold you with my strong right hand.

Isaiah 41:10

He will cover you with his feathers, and under his wings you will find refuge.

Psalm 91: 41

At various times in my process of trying to work all this though, which to be honest has often been spiral, I have gone though periods of hiding, healing and hope. Sometimes they all happen at once in a tangle, and at other times they are a bit more orderly. I will try to explain what I mean.

Hiding

I think when we are over whelmed by pain or grief, we often just want to hide. We do not have the strength to interact with others, or even to think. Hiding can be being covered with a blanket, and refusing to move. It is a way of feeling safe. For me, I could feel safe with God, and I might have a candle lit, and some Christian music on. I think when you are feeling numb or overwhelmed, it is hard to concentrate or read a book. So just listening, can seem the best way of finding nurture, without having to find energy to interact.

The image from Psalm 91, of being able to find refuge with God is a very beautiful one. We can just coorie into the arms of God, and be at peace.

Sometimes we hide, in that we are unavailable to the world, and we need time out. That is not selfish or weak, but necessary. It is a time of lament, acknowledgement of pain, and of moments of intermittent peace. It is part of the journey.

I think another type of hiding, is where we look as if we are functioning, but actually that is just an outward show. We keep going in terms of things we need to do in every day life, but part of us inside is hiding, and outwardly we are just going through the motions. That is just a kind of self protection mechanism. We need to do 'stuff' but our emotional range is limited. We can easily become emotional or angry or upset, so we try not to engage unnecessarily. We put all our emotional energy into looking normal, but when we are tired or unwell, we can be over reactive, to the surprise of friends or colleagues.

I have found reading Gabor Mate's book *When the Body Says No* very informative in this regard. He looks at the connection between our emotional and spiritual wellbeing, and the biological impact this has on our body. He talks about the tension that there is when we try to bury our pain – in denial or repressed anger, and that this stress can cause us to become ill. For example, if we are anxious, our stomach gets sore, or if we are tense, we can have back pain. This reminds us that while we may need to hide for a while, till we are able to process something, that ultimately it is better to be able to share it with a trusted friend, counsellor or therapist.

Brene Brown's work builds on this idea, as she speaks of the importance of honesty, even if we are vulnerable, and this seems so important. Sometimes we are not yet ready to speak, but when we find the courage to share our story, however painful it is, it can diminish shame and bring a healing process. In her TED talk of 2010 she said that vulnerability was the birthplace of great things like of love, belonging, joy, courage, empathy, authenticity and creativity.

This is deeply challenging, but the journey to be more authentic is so liberating. When we are ready, coming out of hiding can be the best move, if we can find safe people to confide in, to hold a space where we can share.

Healing

Ultimately we all want to be whole, at peace with ourselves and with others. It is such a hard thing. There are many wonderful passages in the bible about healing, and Jesus often noticed those whom others had overlooked – the sick child, the woman who was bleeding, the man with leprosy. He wanted them to be whole, not just physically well, but emotionally and spiritually also. Some of the meditations at the end of this book are examples of this kind of journey to wholeness.

For every person the grieving process is very different, and for some people these words might not resonate at all, and this is fine. For others, because of the various combinations of experiences and events, additional work to get well is helpful. For me, there were more layers of hurt and sadness than I realised, and although it has been excruciating to work through, it needed to happen. For everyone, it is good to be self aware, and to look for a supportive community and habits. For many people, a loving family and friends, good listening and care and a supportive community can be enough. However other practices, like spiritual accompaniment, counselling or therapy can also be vital if we feel stuck or lost. Asking for help can make us feel a bit vulnerable, but is actually a sign of strength, to have the awareness that life is tough, and that we might need a safe place to process and to find more specialised support.

The other day I had the opportunity to see a production of 'Les Miserables', which is such a collection of powerful stories and songs about the human condition, of love, betrayal, courage, idealism and so much else.

One of the songs that I really connected with was the song 'Look down' – the song that the slaves sang on the slave ship. The conditions were horrendous, and one of the lyrics is that Jesus doesn't care. Jean Valjean is there for stealing a loaf for his sister when she was starving, and was sentenced to 19 years hard labour. He is described as prisoner 24601, and his name and his humanity is not acknowledged. It is only when the Bishop shows him mercy after he has stolen from him, that he is motivated to start again. Some of the songs from this show, speak to powerfully of themes of forgiveness, suffering, hope and love.

We often feel down because of the injustices in life, and the temptation is conform to other people's expectations of ourselves, and to give up. However a sign of hope, is when we have the interior freedom to look up, to be in the present, and to have a degree of freedom and courage to see that there are other choices. We need to learn to look up, to know that we are not trapped in the past, but can move on.

Gradually, as we get stronger, I guess that there are days when we know we are safe and loved, and that we have freedom to make choices that might be good for us, are days when our healing is less erratic and jaggy, and is more integrated. These moments or days, even if they seem a bit random, are an encouraging sign.

Hope

> Hope is being able to see there is light, despite the darkness.
>
> Desmond Tutu

> I don't think of all the misery, but of the beauty that still remains.
>
> Anne Frank

Hope is such an amazing thing, that somehow after living in days of darkness and pain and tears, there can be days when the sorrow is a bit less, when you can do things without the pain being overwhelming. I think there are always triggers, and for me they when you listen to a veteran's story, or have to answer a question about your life, or you catch a glimpse of an old photograph. These can catapult you back into an old place of trauma and pain. However if the wound had been cleaned, and has had a chance to heal, then it is a bit less sore, and can even be liveable.

And so I write to encourage others. I believe that no one is ever too broken, to be beyond God's mercy and possibilities of healing, no matter what has happened. May we continue to listen, to encourage, to pray and to learn, so we can firm a community of healing and grace for all who struggle.

> Hope is the thing with feathers that perches in the soul and sings the tune without the words, and never stops at all.
>
> Emily Dickinson

And a prayer:

> May the God of hope fill you with all joy and peace as you trust in him, so you may overflow with hope by the power of the Holy Spirit.
>
> Romans 15:13

I have spoken a lot about how individual grief is. People used to say there were different stages of grief – denial, anger, bargaining, depression and acceptance but this seems over simplistic. Writers like Kubler-Ross admit that these are non linear, i.e. that you can experience these repeatedly and in any order and intensity. However every situation is different, and there can be all kinds of reactions to loss. One of the ones it took me ages to identify, was a searching for the lost loved one. Part of you still seems programmed to look for them, even when rationally you know that they are not there. Maybe your car takes you to the hospital they were in, when you are not thinking. Or you just think you caught a glimpse of them in a crowd or in a dream, and there is a sense of being incomplete.

If you feel stuck in your grief, it is always good to talk with a trusted friend or a counsellor. You can talk to your GP, or contact one of the counselling organisations listed in the resources at the end. If you feel you are down and not making any progress, please always talk to some one, and get some additional support.

The writer Ann Voscamp says, 'Shame dies when stories are told in safe places.' And when we are ready, telling our stories, and sharing our concerns, although it takes much courage, can be a very healing thing to do.

If you are struggling with being honest, or making yourself vulnerable, please look at some of the books or podcasts of Brene Brown. She has such a gift for helping us see that being vulnerable takes courage, and can also give other people permission to be honest too.

Whatever place you feel you are in, hiding, healing or hoping, or a unique combination of all three, I offer the following holistic possibilities to explore:

1 Creation – including water

2 Prayer – spiritual resources, spiritual direction, books, bible verses etc. Places – the Ignatian Spirituality Centre in Glasgow, the Bield at Blackruthven near Perth

3 Rest and knowing you are loved

4 Healing for our bodies, exercise, aromatherapy, cranial sacral work, osteopathy

5 Nutrition – herbal

6 Beauty

7 Christian praise music

8 Connection with others, talking, walking, coffee! Listening and sharing stories, acts of hospitality. The idea of the wounded healer.

9 Trauma resources. If trauma has been part of your story, finding people who might help

10 Charitable organisations

A Resources that Help Recovery

1 Creation – especially water!

> He makes me lie down in green pastures, He leads me beside quiet
> waters. He restores my soul.
>
> Psalm 23:2-3a.

The beauty of creation can inspire and comfort and restore. Whether it is
the pattern of a spider's web at your window, or the rhythm of a long walk,
or watching a flower turn from a bud to a bloom. Even a walk in the rain
can be cleansing!

Going for a walk is good for your heart, your weight, releases endorphins
and makes you feel more at peace with the world. Walking in nature, along
a mountain path, the side of the loch or a beach, can help you have space,
appreciate beauty and form, animals and birds, flowers and trees. It helps
you find a different rhythm, if you are able to do this regularly.

If you are weary, sometimes curling up with a soft blanket and soothing
music is ideal. However when your energy levels are better, or you are
frustrated or angry, going for a long walk can be a way of processing some
of that grief or annoyance. Getting into the habit of walking regularly, e.g.
when meeting a friend, can be a great activity, as long as you have the most
appropriate clothes. (This was explored thoroughly in lockdown!!!).

Water of Life

> The ocean is a mighty harmonist.
>
> William Wordsworth

> When anxious, uneasy and bad thoughts come, I go to the sea, and
> the sea drowns them out with its great wide sounds, cleanses me
> with its noise, and imposes a rhythm upon everything in me that is
> bewildered and confused.[13]
>
> Rainer Maria Rilke

A very particular place that can help provide a sense of peace and
grounding is the ocean. I think any space beside water has that negative
ionisation, reflective space and light that can bring cleansing and healing.

---

13 *Letters of Rainer Maria Rilke 1892-1910,* W.W. Norton, 94.

If you carry strong emotions and a lot of empathy, water can be especially soothing, and just walking at a river or loch can bring much peace. Going on a boat trip can also be a great adventure!

Just listening to the lapping of water seems to regulate our heart and our lives, and helps get us back in tune. We get lost in something greater, the heartbeat of the universe, the heart beat of God, and it invites us back into alignment, after trauma and impenetrable grief.

If you have energy, swimming can be another way of losing yourself. For some people swimming in the sea or lochs can be invigorating, although it is always good to get wise advice first. I think that water can be sacramental, speaking to us of the cleansing power of baptism, and the abundant and infinite love of God which refreshes and supports and inspires.

2 Prayer

Is prayer your steering wheel or your spare tyre?

Corrie Ten Boom

God speaks in the silence of the heart. Listening is the beginning of prayer.

Mother Theresa

When you are feeling low or are grieving, then it can be difficult to pray. Sometimes we need to ask others to pray for us, and to carry us, when we are finding it hard to concentrate.

In days like these, it can be useful to use some of the prayer and meditation apps online. *Abide, Lectio 365*, and *Pray as you go* are three examples of different kinds of apps that can be downloaded onto your phone. They are free, although *Abide* has a more comprehensive paid version also. These apps offered guided prayer and meditation for each day, so you can listen if you find it harder to read. There can also be meditations on particular topics, if you cannot sleep or are feeling anxious.

At the end of this section there is a selection of inspiring verses, which can be a great focus for prayer.

Journalling can be a good way of expressing what is going on in your life also, just taking time to write down, what you are struggling with, and what God is doing. These are all just suggestions, but it is worth exploring them, to see if any are helpful.

Places

There are many resources on prayer, and spiritual accompaniment can also help. Going to a Retreat Centre like The Bield at Blackruthven can also help to find attentive listening, a loving presence and peace.

Thinking of the Ignatian Spirituality Centre, the Ignatian process of using the Examen might help, where at the end of each day you look to see where God was at work in your day and you give thanks, and that you also notice where you struggled, and ask what you might learn from it. This is an oversimplification, but it is worth looking at Ignatian practices, as well as the many others available, to see what might help. At the end of the book, there is a list of verses to browse, which might be an encouragement and focus for prayer. Exploring spiritual accompaniment can also be a way to reflect on how we pray, and to find encouragement as to how we connect with God.

At times, prayer can be intercession for loved ones, asking God to bless them and keep them safe. At other times, prayer can be resting in God's presence, and listening for his voice. Building that relationship with Jesus in prayer is a blessing, and there is rich seam of grace and healing that flows from it. There is so much to explore. There can be dry times, when our prayers hit the ceiling, but then other times when we feel so close to God, that we just want to stay in his presence forever.

> Prayer should not be regarded as a duty to be performed, but rather as a privilege to be enjoyed, a rare delight which is always revealing some new beauty.
>
> E M Bounds

3 Rest

> In the inner stillness where meditation leads, the Spirit secretly anoints the soul and heals our deepest wounds.
>
> John of the Cross

Resting and knowing that we are loved. Rather than reading about it - this is one to do! Whether it is going to bed early, having an afternoon nap or just day dreaming, we all need space in our lives, just to be!

Part of rest, can also having spaces to rest in. It could be a comfortable chair, or a place near a window. Sometimes we can pick up an inspirational book like *The Swallow, the Owl and the Sandpiper* – words of courage, wisdom and spirit. Or we might read a beautiful book like Tish Harrison Warren's books, *Liturgy of the Ordinary* or *A Prayer in the Night* – they are gentle, and we can just read a few lines, and then rest.

Making space can be part of creating a restful environment. When I was busy with family, caring and working, there were areas of the house that became a bit disorganised, and visually seeing that there was excess 'stuff' didn't help my sense of wellbeing. It felt overwhelming and heavy. I was fortunate to meet a wonderful 'declutterer' who helped me learn how to enjoy and cherish the items that are important to me, and to let others go. I think there are stages of life when we desire to re-order 'things'. Especially around bereavement, I think there can be a process of readjusting, whether it is photographs, clothes or bigger items. There are many issues about timing – so this only when you feel ready. For me, I benefited enormously from a decluttering experience, so that in rooms, 'stuff' and purpose became more integrated, and this brought me peace. The resulting space and light gave me opportunity to feel more spacious in my spirit also. I need to do this regularly, to work through different symbolic memories from my life and also parts of my house, so that what is left is what is most significant.

Physically, we need rest to save us from exhaustion and burn out. Emotionally we need space. And spiritually, we crave restoration. There are many restorative images – of a child with a parent, a sheep in green pastures, the harmony of the lion and the lamb lying down together.

> In place of our exhaustion and spiritual fatigue, God will give us rest. All he asks is that we come to him . . . that we spend a while thinking about him, meditating on him, talking to him, listening in silence, occupying ourselves with him – totally and thoroughly lost in the hiding place of His presence.
>
> Chuck Swindoll

Eugene Peterson in *The Message* offers us a brilliant paraphrase of Jesus, words in Matthew 11:28-30:

> Come to me. Get away with me and you'll recover your life. I'll show you how to take a real rest. Walk with me and work with me – watch how I do it. Learn the unforced rhythms of grace.

I think the secret of resting, is to cultivate these 'unforced rhythms of grace', to listen to our souls, our bodies and to God, as to when to rest, when to play, when to work. This rhythm will be different in different seasons of our lives. There are times when watching boxed sets and eating ice cream are a good distraction! There are times when we are weary – we need less stimulation from rubbish TV and social media, more healthy food and earlier nights. There are times when we need to face up to difficult conversations and to set out in a new direction. Being gentle with ourselves, and having healthy patterns of rest and quiet all contribute to our health, in whatever place we find ourselves.

In his book *The Dance of Life*, Henri Nouwen describes our struggle just to turn off the inner voices and struggles and be at peace, and reminds us that the prayers of Jesus to his heavenly Father came from a silence we need to cultivate, letting go our inner debate with myself and everyone else, and just listening to God.

4 Healing for our bodies

As we have already seen, when we are stressed, off balance, traumatised or grieving, it is always good to consider how our bodies are doing, as well as our souls! As well as all the other ideas offered earlier, there might be other things to consider. Going to our GP for a check up is always a good thing to do. If we are troubled by painful memories, grief or feeling of being overwhelmed of exhaustion, then it can be useful to talk to some-one trained in aromatherapy, sacral cranial work, osteopathy, massage, capacitar etc.

Breath work is a great thing to explore, as it can soothe the nervous system, calm anxiety and bring relaxation. It is calming to take deep breathes, and especially a shorter breath in, and then a longer out – it stimulates the vagus nerve, which can result in a more relaxed feel, and cause a physiological response of lower heartrate and blood pressure. People remember this by saying the words 'hot chocolate' to breathe in sharply, and out in a longer breath. Another simple way of doing this is to breathe in for 3 counts, hold the breath for 4 counts, and exhale for 5 counts. There are good resources about this on you tube. It is interesting to notice the overlap between different spiritual practices, like saying prayers and liturgy together in community, and the impact that this rhythm has of encouraging slow deep breathing, and helping the body relax into this calmer more meditative state.

Many things can lift and ameliorate our mood, especially scent, for example lavender for your pillow to help you sleep. If you are tossing and turning at night, a relaxing fragrance can really help. Favourite colognes or perfumes can give you confidence if you are walking into a stressful situation, and can be seen as an anointing. Lemon can boost your mood, or rosemary can lower fatigue. Aromatherapy oils, used carefully, can help if you feel anxious or stressed.

5 Nutrition

Let food be your medicine, your medicine shall be your food.

Hippocrates

Often when we have been a carer or are finding life hard, we forget to eat properly, and this impacts on how we feel and how our body functions. The temptation is to go for fast food, or things that are easy to prepare but have little nutrition in them! Reviewing our nutrition is part of becoming more well, to eat more healthily, to consider nutritional supplements. Looking at herbal teas and medicines can also be useful (as long as you ok this with a GP first in case of any medical interactions) – a gentle and natural way of finding balance and health. A peppermint tea can be good for digestion, or chamomile to help you relax.

It is amazing how a deficiency in something can impact your life. For a while, I was trying to be more plant based in my eating, and didn't realise that I was missing out on protein, and this made me more tired. We all have different ways of coping with stress, so it can be worth reviewing our eating habits, to see if there are ways we can better look after our body.

If you are a gardener, and can grow your own herbs, even better! Gardening can also be a very therapeutic thing in itself, and good for the soul.

6 Beauty

Our environment can play a big part in our wellbeing, and if we have opportunity to have beauty around us, that can keep us connected with things that are positive and a blessing.

When we look at something beautiful, whether it is a bird in the garden, a striking picture in an art gallery (maybe a van Gogh), or a great theatre production, it can be mesmerising. It helps us forget our current pain and emptiness, and remind us that there is something greater. I think these experiences can be quite ethereal, expanding our imagination and inspiring us to be full of awe. Somehow it seems to rewire us and bring healing.

Reading writers like John O'Donohue can re-orientate us, when we have lost our way.

> The human soul is hungry for beauty; we seek it everywhere – in landscape, music, art, clothes, furniture, gardening, companionship, love, religion and in ourselves. No-one would desire not to be beautiful. When we experience the Beautiful, there is a sense of homecoming. Some of our most wonderful memories are of beautiful places where we felt immediately at home. We feel most alive in the presence of the Beautiful for it meets the needs of our soul.[14]

> Frequently, beauty is playful like dancing sunlight, it cannot be predicted, and in the most unlikely scene or situation can suddenly emerge. This spontaneity and playfulness often subverts our self-importance and throws our plans and intentions into disarray. Without intending it, we find ourselves coming alive with a sense of celebration and delight. The pedestrian sequence of a working day breaks, a new door opens and the heart recognizes the silent majesty of the ordinary. The things we never notice, like health, friends and love, emerge from their subdued presence and stand out in their true radiance as gifts we could never have earned or achieved. Beauty.[15]

I think there is something about beauty, whether it is the words of a friend, or the presence of God, that can breathe new life into us, just for a moment. Every time we choose to appreciate a beautiful moment, however small, it is like a stepping stone on the road to recovery, a square restored to the quilt that covers us each night.

---

14 John O'Donohue, *Divine Beauty: The Invisible Embrace*, Pengin Random House, 2.
15 O'Donohue, *Divine Beauty*, 22.

7 Christian praise music

> Beautiful music is the art of the prophets that can calm the agitations
> of the soul. It is one of the most magnificent and delightful presents
> that God gives us.
>
> Martin Luther

I remember many years ago, listening to a speaker who was telling his life story, and shared about being abused as a boy. He had a very difficult road to recovery, and he spoke about how in some parts of his life, all he could do was listen to praise music for days at a time. Somehow something in his spirit aligned with the words and spirit of the music, and helped him when he was struggling with destructive thoughts and dark memories.

At the time, when I heard this, I thought it was a bit dramatic, but I understand it better now. I think when we are hurting and in pain, we cannot always think rationally and work things out. We need to find a way to regulate first, and music can be incredibly healing and positive.

We all have different musical tastes, whether it is classical music, or traditional hymns, or modern praise music. They can all speak to us in different ways, reminding us we are loved, inspiring our emotions, soothing our souls. Christian music has another dimension, for it can lead us into the presence of God, which also reminds us that we are not alone, and bringing a deep sense of connection with the Creator of the universe, and bring refreshment and peace.

For me, it was praise music that really speaks to me, and especially on my worst days. And so I offer some of these songs in the specific resources section. I had play lists for sorrowful days, days of exhaustion, days of slight hope, days of setback, days of doubting etc. I have put a selection of songs and bands on here, to give you a place to start, to see if these songs help in any way.

8 Connection

Particularly when we are suffering, we often need to work things out ourselves. We can be well supported by counsellors, family or friends, but we still need to come to terms with things. This can seem like lonely work.

Connection can make all the difference. For me, I think of the connection with God as making all the difference. I can share with God the cries of my heart, and know that he has a purpose for me, even in my brokenness.

One of my favourite authors is Henri Nouwen, for he wrote about things with an emotional honesty about spiritual intimacy and grace. He speaks about us all being wounded healers, and this can be a very purposeful way of making sense of what has happened to us.

He speaks of how all people are wounded – alienated or lonely or afraid at times, and that this is part of the human condition. The acceptance of our common struggles however, brings human connection. He talks of community being formed in this way,

> when loneliness is among the chief wounds of the minister, hospitality can convert that wound into a source of healing. Concentration prevents the minister from burdening others with his pain and allows him to accept his wounds as helpful teachers of his own and his neighbours condition. Community arises where the sharing of pain takes place, not as a stifling form of self complaint, but as a recognition of God's saving promises.[16]

Nouwen had a great gift of talking of suffering and brokenness as part of the human condition, and that when we are honest about this, it can be the source of our connection and healing.

He also spoke about the power of love, to help people feel strong and inspired. He said that each person needs to claim their true identity as the 'beloved of God'. He speaks of Jesus' baptism, when Jesus is told that he is loved by the Father, and he says:

> Jesus revealed that we sinful, broken human beings are invited to that same communion that Jesus lived, that we are beloved sons and daughters of God, just as he is the beloved son . . .[17]

These quotations remind us of the power of connection with love and with God, but God also wants to bless us with connection in community. We all have a responsibility to help form such a community, even through qualities such as vulnerability and humility.

---

16 Henri Nouwen, *The Wounded Healer,* Darton Longman and Todd 2014, 99.
17 Henri Nouwen, *Here and Now Living in the Spirit*, Darton, Longman and Todd 1994, 122-3.

As we have seen in Bruce Perry's book *Born to Love* just being seen or appreciated by one person, can make all the difference. Connection and love do change everything.

At its best, living in Christian community, can be also be a life giving experience, where we prayerfully encourage each other on.

> The word 'Christian' means different things to different people. To one person it means a stiff, upright, inflexible way of life, colorless and unbending. To another it means a risky, surprised-filled adventure, lived tiptoe at the edge of expectation . . . if we get our information from the biblical material, there is no doubt that the Christian life is a dancing, leaping, daring life.[18]

This vision of the Christian life in an authentic community is again so healing.

9 Trauma resources

This is probably the hardest section to speak about, because I am speaking only from anecdotes and experience, not with a professional expertise. I think I am wary to say much on this complex topic, as there is so much I do not understand.

However, the reason I keep speaking is because I listen to so many people who have gone through intense and dark experiences of trauma, who are looking for healing, and there seems so little to help.

For me, understanding the relationship between trauma, mind, spirit and body really helped, and Bessel van der Kolk's book *The Body Keeps the Score* transformed my understanding. Other books that helped were Bruce Perry's book with Oprah Winfrey *What Happened to You* and *The Boy Who was Raised as a Dog*. Having a framework of understanding has made such a difference.

There are many helpful Christian books on suffering also, such as Philip Yancey's *Where is God When it Hurts?*, Jennifer Rees Larcombe's *Beauty from Ashes* and more recent books like Ann Voscamp's *One Thousand Gifts* and Lysa Terkeurst *It's not Supposed to Be This Way*. I think it is a

---

18 Eugene H. Peterson, cited in *God's Message for Each Day: Wisdom from the Word of God: a 365 Day Devotional 2020*, Thomas Nelson, 358.

very personal thing as to which author resonates with you, and it is worth listening to different voices. It is ok to disagree, and then try someone else!

There are also many helpful practical approaches, about breathing, food, body work etc, as previously mentioned

I don't always know people who embrace this kind of approach to trauma in Scotland. Many organisations do great work in specific fields, but it can be hard to find the best path that people can access for support, as what one person finds to be supportive, another feels is less so.

Support may also come from:

Trauma therapies like EMDR (Eye Movement Desensitisation and Reprocessing)

www.capacitar.org

Osteopathic support and cranial osteopathy – e.g. Anna Potter, 34 George Street, Glasgow, text 07734 439348

See also the books on trauma listed under 'Spiritual Resources for the Weary' later in this section.

10 Signposts to other organisations

Epilepsy Connections, Suites 129-135, 50 Wellington Street, Glasgow G2 6HJ, 0141 248 4125

Community Veterans Support, 840-860 Govan Road, Glasgow G51 3UU (previously known as the Coming Home Centre), 0141 237 8830

Quiet Waters, 2 Glasgow Rd, Camelon, Falkirk FK1 4HJ, 01324 630643

Tom Allan Centre, 23 Elmbank Street, Glasgow G2 4PB, 0141 221 1535

Scottish Men's Sheds Association, Banchory Business Centre, Banchory, Aberdeenshire AB31 5ZU, 07397 382533 (phone to find your local shed)

The Bield at Blackruthven, Blackruthven House, Perth PH1 1PY, 01738 583238

Healing for the Heart Counselling, 07397 984288

Ignatian Spirituality Centre, 35 Scott Street, Glasgow

Living Life (NHS telephone service), 0800 3289655

The Spark 0808 802 2088 (counselling and mental health support for individuals, families and young people)

The Samaritans, 116 123.

Christian Healing Ministries, Jacksonville, Florida, USA.

Richmond's Hope in Glasgow and Edinburgh, https://www. richmondshope.org.uk

There are also useful Blogs/Facebook sites, such as:

The Unravelling by Kelli Bachara

Anam Cara Ministries

Hope for the Broken Hearted

Black Sheep Counselling

Contemplative Monk

A Modern Day Ruth

Hope for the Brokenhearted

Midwives of the Soul

Marika Osuji – Heartbeat of the Father

Songs of the Beloved – words and art for the soul

B Spiritual Resources for the Weary

When you are sad, feeling upset or helpless, or trying to care for someone who is unwell or has an incapacity, you can become exhausted and drained. And so I offer some further resources that encouraged me – they might not be for everyone, but at key moments, they spoke to my heart.

1 BOOKS

Some books I happened to be reading (some already mentioned in the book), which helped in different ways

Streams in the Desert – Lettie Cowman

Healing Every Day – Mary De Murtha

Hinds' Feet on High Places – Hannah Hurnard

When the Heart Waits – Sue Monk Kidd

The Other Side of Chaos – Margaret Silf

Lessons of the Heart – Patricia Livingston.

Divine Beauty – John O'Donohue

The Blessing of Tears – Julie Sheldon

Praying our Goodbyes – Joyce Rupp

Beauty from Ashes – Jennifer Rees Larcombe

God Loves Broken People – Sheila Walsh

Prayer in the Night – Tish Harrison Warren

Liturgy of the Ordinary – Tish Harrison Warren

Sensible Shoes – a novel by Sharon Garlough Brown

The Cure for Sorrow – Jan Richardson

Learning to Walk in the Dark – Barbara Brown Taylor

One Thousand Gifts – Ann Voscamp

The Swallow, the Owl and the Sandpiper – poems and prose compiled by Claire Maitland for the Sandpiper Trust

The Boy, the Mole, the Fox and the Horse – Charles Mackesy

Books particularly on trauma

The Body Keeps the Score – Bessel van der Kolk

Born for Love – Maia Szalavitz and Bruce Perry

The Boy Who Thought He was a Dog – Bruce Perry

What Happened to You? – Bruce Perry and Oprah Winfrey

When the Body Says No – Gabor Mate

Healing Your Lost Inner Child – Robert Jackman

A trauma informed practice toolkit is available from the Scottish Government (15th March 2021). It advocates safety, trust, choice, collaboration and empowerment.

Lovely books for children

For wee ones (4-8):

Mindful Monkey, Happy Panda – Lauren Alderfer

I am Stronger than Anger – Elizabeth Cole

For older children:

The Invisible String (and workbook) – Dana Wyss and Patrice Karst

Thoughts to Make Your Heart Sing – Sally Lloyd-Jones

2 BIBLE

Verses that encouraged me during times of illness and grieving

Weeping may come in the night, but joy comes in the morning.

Psalm 30:5

My tears have been my food, both day and night.

Psalm 42:3

When I am afraid, I will trust in you.

Psalm 56:3

Take courage, it is I. Do not be afraid.

Matthew 14:27

My grace is sufficient for you, for my power is made perfect in weakness.

2 Corinthians 12:9

Through deep waters, I will be with you.

Isaiah 43:2

We walk by faith, not by sight.

2 Corinthians 5:7

My soul is overwhelmed to the point of death. Stay here and keep watch with me.

Matthew 26:38

My times are in your hands.

Psalm 31:15

For our light and momentary troubles are achieving for us an eternal glory that far outweighs them all. So we fix our eyes not on what is seen, but on what is unseen, since what is seen is temporary, but what is unseen is eternal.

2 Corinthians 4:17-18

The Spirit of the Sovereign LORD is on me,
    because the LORD has anointed me
  to proclaim good news to the poor.
He has sent me to bind up the brokenhearted,
    to proclaim freedom for the captives
      and release from darkness for the prisoners,
    to proclaim the year of the LORD's favour
    and the day of vengeance of our God,
to comfort all who mourn,
    and provide for those who grieve in Zion—
to bestow on them a crown of beauty
    instead of ashes,
the oil of joy
    instead of mourning,
and a garment of praise
    instead of a spirit of despair.

Isaiah 63:1-3

Sorrowing but always rejoicing.

2 Corinthians 6:10

In quietness and trust is your strength.

Isaiah 30:15

Whether we live or die, we belong to the Lord.

Romans 14:8

Father, if you are willing, remove this cup from me, yet not my will but your will.

Luke 22:42

Wait for the Lord, be strong and take heart, and wait for the Lord.

Psalm 27:14

Why are you downcast, O my soul, why so disturbed within me? Put your hope in God, for I will yet praise him, my saviour and my God.

Psalm 42:5

My flesh and my heart may fail, but God is the strength of my heart and my portion forever.

Psalm 73:26

He will cover you with his feathers;
under his wings you will find refuge;
his faithfulness is a shield and rampart.

Psalm 91:4

Those who hope in the LORD will renew their strength. They will soar on wings like eagles; they will run and not grow weary, they will walk and not be faint.

Isaiah 40:31

He was despised and rejected by men, a man of sorrows and familiar with suffering, like one from whom men hide their faces, he was despised and we esteemed him not.

Surely he took up our infirmities, and carried our sorrows, yet we considered him stricken by God, smitten by him and afflicted.

But he was pierced for our transgressions, he was crushed for our iniquities, the punishment that brought us peace was upon him, and by his wounds we are healed.

Isaiah 53:3-5

The Lord your God is with you, he is mighty to save. He will take delight in you, he will quiet you with his love, he will rejoice over you with singing.

Zephaniah 3:17

Jesus went though Galilee, teaching in their synagogues, preaching the good news of the kingdom, and healing every disease and sickness amongst the peoples.

Matthew 4:23

Do not be afraid – you are worth more than many sparrows.

Matthew 10:31

Come to me, all you who are weary and heavy burdened, and I will give you rest. Take my yoke upon you and learn from me, for I am gentle and humble in heart, and you will find rest for my souls. For my yoke is easy and my burden is light.

Matthew 11:28-30

Take courage. It is I – do not be afraid.

Matthew 14:27

Jesus got up, rebuked the wind and said to the waves, 'Quiet, be still.'

Mark 4:39

Jesus wept.

John 11:35

Praise be to the God and Father of the Lord Jesus Christ, the Father of compassion and the God of all comfort, who comforts us in all our troubles, so we can comfort those in any trouble with the comfort we ourselves have received from God. For just as the sufferings of Christ flow into our lives, so also through Christ, our comfort overflows.

2 Corinthians 1:3-5

May the God of hope fill you with all joy and peace as you trust in him, so that you may overflow with hope by the power of the Holy Spirit.

Romans 15:13

Praise be to the God and Father of our Lord Jesus Christ, who has blessed us in the heavenly realms with every spiritual blessing in Christ.

Ephesians 1:3

Do not be anxious about everything, but in everything, by prayer and petition, with thanksgiving, present your requests to God.

Philippians 4:6-7

Be joyful always, pray continually, give thanks in all circumstances, for this is God's will for you in Jesus Christ.

1 Thessalonians 5:16-18

May the Lord direct your hearts into God's love and Christ's perseverance.

2 Thessalonians 3:5

3 SONGS

Songs to listen to when you feel at the bottom of the pit. On these darkest days, these artists (and many more) became like my friends on the journey!

When you want to be left alone to be miserable – Mandisa, 'Just Cry'

Trying to trust in the midst of pain and despair – Tim Hughs, 'When the Tears Fall'

Just miserable – Rend Collective, 'Weep with Me'

The idea that after all the tears, there could still be love – Andrew Peterson, 'After the Last Tear 'Falls'

In the deepest darkness, there could one day be light – Andrew Peterson, 'The Dark Before the Dawn'

When you feel that you have failed, and you want to give up – Andrew Peterson, 'Be Kind to Yourself'

When the world feels hostile, being with God is our safe house – Andrew Peterson, 'My One Safe Place'

When you are hurting – Jason Gray, 'Love Will Have the Final Word'

In the midst of frustration and nothing making sense – Jason Gray, 'Even This Will be Made Beautiful

When you feel scared – Rob Gardner, 'Nothing to fear'

When nothing works, and you just have to rely on God – Hillsong, 'I Surrender'

When feeling like I am tired and inadequate, and can't do anymore – Lauren Daigle, 'You Say'

When feeling like the world has no meaning – Lauren Daigle, 'Love Like This'

When so tired, you can't stand up – Lauren Daigle, 'Rescue'

When I am hurting, please sit with me and don't give me platitudes – Jason Gray, 'Not Right Now'

When you are exhausted, and nothing makes any sense – Laura Story, 'Nearness'

Even when things fall apart, again, and God is calling us to trust him – Casting Crowns, 'Praise You in the Storm'

When you have lost hope, and you need encouragement to keep going – Casting Crowns, 'Courageous'

When you are tired just trying to support everyone else – Casting Crowns, 'Just be Held'

When you have waited so long, but part of you still hopes – Danny Cokey, – 'Haven't Seen it Yet?'

When you are too tired to do anything but rest in God's love – Elevation Worship, 'With You (Paradoxology)'

When the world seems to be falling apart, God keeps us safe – Elevation Worship, 'For a Moment'

God never forsakes us – Matt Redman, 'Never Once'

Can something good come from the pain? – Laura Story, 'Blessings'

I am trying too hard, and its not working – Laura Story, 'Grace'

I don't need to pretend everything is ok, when I am with God – Laura Story, 'Peace'

When I feel afraid, your love crashes over me – Bethel Music, 'You Make Me Brave' (live)

God has written a song just for me – Bethel Music, 'We Dance' (live)

God discovers me in my brokenness and brings healing – Jason Gray, 'Learning to be Found'

When I am so miserable and nothing is working out, I still trust – Mercy Me, 'Even If'

Hope of beauty from the ashes – The Afters, 'Broken Hallelujah'

Remembering a loved one – Casting Crowns, 'The Only Scars in Heaven'

Whatever happens, even if I fail, God still keeps hold of me – Laura Story, 'He Will not Let Go'

God is still here – Michael Card, 'Never Will I Leave You'

When I feel lost and alone – Michael Card, 'I Will Bring You Home'

You are faithful, even when I struggle – Sarah Reeves, 'Faithful'

Let me not be distracted from loving You, God – Sarah Reeves, 'Just Want You'

When people around you are discouraging – Francesca Battistelli, 'Giants Fall'

When prayer is not answered, |I need to still cling on – Lauren Daigle, 'Trust in You'

When I am hurting, I don't need to move, for God seeks me out – Laura Story, 'You Came Running'

Making the right choice – Yvonne Lyon, 'Again'

When you feel alone – Yvonne Lyon, 'Lonely Road'

When you are struggling – Yvonne Lyon, 'All is not lost'

In the midst of the mess – Yvonne Lyon, 'I am loved'

When things don't make sense, but at least you are still here – Mercy Me, 'The Hurt and the Healer'

When it seems too long to wait – Stoneleigh Worship Band, 'We Have Sung our Songs'

Waiting and trusting – Laura Story, 'Whisper'

Don't ever give up – J.J. Heller, 'Don't Give Up Too Soon'

When we are so very tired – Ellie Holcomb, 'I Will Carry You'

Even in the midst of darkness – Lydia Laird, 'Hallelujah Even Here'

Songs to listen to, when a little light seems possible

Even yet, something good might come from this – Nichole Nordeman, 'Something Out of Me'

Every detail can bring meaning – Nichole Nordeman, 'Every Mile Mattered'

There is something more to this, than just suffering: maybe there can be a positive direction – Nichole Nordeman, 'Listen to Your Life'

Out of brokenness, there can be new beginnings – Danny Cokey, 'Tell Your Heart to Beat Again'
Just because you feel desolate and broken, doesn't mean you are not loved – Danny Cokey, 'Wanted'

Desiring to tell your story, but not knowing where to start – Nicole Nordeman, 'Sound of surviving'

When you need to be reminded you have stamina – Matthew West, 'Never Give Up'

God is still faithful, even when it doesn't feel like it – Natalie Grant, 'Never Miss a Beat'

In the midst of it all, there is still hope – Danny Cokey, 'Hope in Front of Me'

Trusting – Lou Fellingham, 'Wholly Yours'

Trusting when there is no sense, again – Lauren Daigle, 'Trust in You'

Relief: it is ok to let go and to trust – Laura Story, 'I Can Just Be Me'

God gives me strength and courage to get out of the boat – We the Kingdom, 'Dancing on the waves' (live)

There is some sense in it all even when it doesn't seem to make sense! – Jason Gray, 'Nothing is Wasted'

Somehow I am still a real person – Jason Gray, 'Be Your Own Kind of Beautiful'

When I don't know who I am anymore: only a carer – Jason Gray, 'Remind Me Who I Am'

When I feel weak, you call me back to your side – Hillsong United, 'Even When it Hurts'

God can breathe life into my tired soul, and give me new life – Jason Gray, 'New Way to Live'

After everything, God can form something new out of my life – Jason Gray, 'Love's not Done with You'

I have learned from this, as God has put me back together – Jason Gray, 'I will rise again'

When things are tough, God still holds our hand – Jason Gray, 'A Way to See in the Dark'

God gives me strength to persevere (and dance) – Mandisa, 'Overcomer'

Scars and brokenness tell their own story – Mandisa, 'What Scars Are For'

God is creating something new out of the pain – Casting Crowns, 'In the Hands of the Potter'

In the midst of it all, you call me to still know joy – Mandisa, 'I Hope You Dance'

God is amazing, in the midst of it all – Laura Story, 'Extraordinary'

Sometimes we need to speak, welcome or not – Best Friends, 'Born for This (Esther)'

It is ok to be me – Francesca Battistelli, 'Free to Be Me'

I need to have the courage to tell our story – Francesca Battistelli, 'Write Your Story'

In the midst of it all, the miracle is that God still loves us – Lauren Daigle, 'Love Like This'

God is close to me when I feel broken – The Afters, 'Forever and Always'

Waiting and worshipping – Cody Carnes, 'Nothing Else'

God somehow never lets us down – Hawk Nelson, 'Never Let You Down'

When we are really tired again – J.J. Heller, 'You Already Know'

Poignant but hopeful songs (some even with a beat!)

Somehow maybe things might work out – Newsboys, 'Symphony'

A sense of perspective – Colton Dixon, 'Through All of It'

A feeling of being forgiven and freedom – Matthew West, 'Grace Upon Grace'

Relief from worry – Hawk Nelson, 'Weightless'

Noticing the light – The Afters, 'Life is Beautiful'

Finding more of my identity – Anthem Lights, 'Who I'm Meant to Be'

It's ok to be me! – Leanna Crawford, 'Crazy, Beautiful You'

It's ok to do something new – Rick Pino, 'Pioneer'

Telling others of the beauty of faith is ok – Amy Grant, 'A Woman'

A way forward – Hawk Nelson, 'Live Like You're Loved'

Acceptance of today – The Afters, 'Breathe in, Breathe out'

God's love holds us – Ryan Stevenson, 'Eye of the Storm'

5 MEDICAL

What are the kind of questions that need to be asked?

- What rights do patients and their families have, when the patient has epilepsy, brain injury or lacks capacity? Here is what you will need to do, and you should be confident about doing it:

- Ask for information about your loved one's condition.

- Ask to speak to the doctor about what is happening, what is going on, what the plan is? To question why?

- Tell the doctor/nurse what the context is and what your concern is – you know your loved one's history, in a way the medical staff do not.

- On a ward, ask to speak to the consultant, and ask for information. Also make clear if you have power of attorney, to make sure that this is marked on the notes, and to ensure that there are arrangements for good communication. Keep telling everyone you are POA.

- Feed in information that might not be available – e.g. to check their record of medication is up to date.

- If you are POA, you can ask to see the notes.

- If you are not sure, you can ask for a second opinion.

It can also be good, if you are able, to take some-one with you, to help listen to all that's being said. Writing things down, to help remember, is also a good idea. Sometimes doctors and nurses use medical terms, so never be afraid to ask what they mean, and to ask if they could explain what is meant.

6 ORGANISATIONS and WEBSITES

In addition to those listed earlier:

Read the Charter of Patient Rights and Responsibilities on your local NHSS website.

Patient Advice and Support Service, 0800 917 2127, offers confidential support and advice on health related matters in NHS Scotland.

Local patients support groups.

Care opinion UK – feed your story to this non profit feedback platform for health and social care, to make services better.

Scottish Independent Advocacy Alliance, 0131 510 9410

Specific Veteran's resources.

'Veteran's Champions' are officials who have volunteered to support veterans within the NHS and local councils. They are worth contacting for support. All veterans should have the code 13JY on their notes for NHS care, which activates a covenant for priority treatment for all ex service personnel.

Veteran's Gateway Tel 08088021212 – signposts veterans and their families to different types of support. (This could include, eg Combat Stress, Veterans with dogs, Coming Home centre etc)

Section 5: MEDITATIONS, and a FINAL WORD

Lying at the roadside *(inspired by Luke 10:23-37)*

I am lying on the ground, bruised and beaten,
I have no energy, I can't remember where it was that I was going.
I was on the path, and suddenly it all changed,
In just a few blurry moments, everything was taken from me,
And I was wounded, lost, the world became upside down.

I didn't see their faces,
I just felt what they had done,
And I was in shock, too numb to move, or even to cry out.
I felt so very helpless and sore.

It was hot, and the sun was beating down,
And I heard a noise, and thought someone is coming to help me,
But then although I heard footsteps,
Somehow they never came.

And I felt worse, for not only was I helpless,
But I wasn't even worth anyone's notice.

And then later, it happened again,
Someone seemed to be coming,
But their pace never faltered,
Did they not see me?

And then, much much later,

I heard footsteps again,

But by this time I didn't even hope,

I was too weak, I felt beyond help.

To my astonishment, this person came over,

He had compassion on me,

Although he did not know me,

He saw me.

He gave me something to drink,

With the most fragrant ointment,

He gently bound up my wounds,

And lifted me onto his donkey.

I tried to say sorry, sorry to put you out,

I know this is not fair on you,

But he just smiled, and supported me, and kept me upright

Along that bumpy track.

Every part of me ached,

But it was ok, because I was seen,

I was cared for,

And I knew that all would be well.

Grace for the ashamed *(inspired by John 8:1-11)*

How I got here, I am not so sure.

It all happened so quickly,

He seemed so charming, so beguiling,

And I was captured by his charms.

I knew it was wrong, and so when the men broke in,
Screaming and pulling us apart,
I knew why this was happening,
And I felt humiliated, degraded.

I never saw him again,
As I was led outside,
And there was a crowd of people
Calling for me to be stoned to death for what I had done.
They raised their hands,
I was terrified, I couldn't move,
I just thought this is what I deserved.

There was a young Rabbi there
I had not seen him before,
He seemed to be writing in the sand.

He asked the one who was not guilty
To throw the first stone,
And I was prepared to die,
What more could I expect.

But one by one, they lowered their arms
And slunk away,
Till only the Rabbi was left.

I waited, my spirit was shrinking,
Waiting for judgement
But he said, 'Daughter, go and sin no more.'

Tears came to my eyes,
He knew I was a sinner,
Yet he called me 'Daughter'
He spoke to me with grace
And I was given a second chance.

Hope when all hope seemed gone *(inspired by Luke 8:40-56)*

I was some-one who tried to do the right thing
To look after my wife and family,
To provide for my household.
I had a busy job,
To look after so many employees,
And it was tough,
I needed authority to keep things together.

And so it was so unjust when my daughter became ill.
At first it didn't seem too bad,
But then she got worse,
And I was at my wits end.
I wasn't a religious man,
But I cried out to God,
And I was just so desperate,
I would have done anything to help my daughter.
When I looked into her eyes,
And saw her fear and bewilderment
I just wanted to help, to make things better.

I heard there was a teacher of the law in town,
That he was a miracle worker,
And I sent my servant to ask him to make my girl better.
I didn't want to leave her bedside.
I knew that he spoke with authority
His teaching was different from all the rest,
It was distinctive, even powerful.

But then she died.
I was devastated, nothing had worked,
Her life had been taken away.

The teacher said that he would help,

And she woke up.

I believe now, I think I would have believed even if she had not come
    back to life,

For the Teacher heard me,

And he was there,

And I was full of gratitude,

And deep thanksgiving.

The love of God is for all,

Even those on the fringes,

Nothing can separate us from Him,

Whatever happens.

Acceptance and healing   *(inspired by Matthew 8:1-4)*

I had had leprosy for so many years,

It looked ugly, and when one bit of my skin seemed improved,

Another bit became infected.

When I looked at my limbs,

I didn't recognise myself,

Just bandages and deformities.

And that wasn't the worst bit,

The greatest horror

Was that other people

Judged me to be unclean,

That somehow I was outside the grace of God.

The community ran me out of town

To the caves,

With the others with skin diseases.

We tried to help each other out,
To share the meagre supplies,
But it was a lonely life,
I was rejected and lived life on the edge.

Then the Healer came to town,
And he laid his hand on me
And said that I should go to see the priest,
And that I would be clean.

To be honest, I hesitated,
And wondered if he knew what he was doing.
Hadn't I been rejected enough,
Why would I go back to the priest again
To endure that torment and judgement.

But I went, and a miracle happened,
For my skin was healed, it was restored and smooth,
And I was whole again.
I was accepted, and I was healed,
And so I went back to say thankyou,
For he had changed my life forever.

The aching heart of a parent *(inspired by Luke 15:11-32)*

The sense of yearning and loss was palpable,
You could be talking about whatever topic,
But there was a wisfulness in their eyes,
And you could tell that their heart was somewhere else.

It was so, ever since their child left
And the pain and hurt and uncertainty were so deep,
Would I ever see them again,
Why did they need to leave,
Tears and anguish.

And so the parent keeps replaying everything in their mind
Wishing that small detail could have been otherwise,
Yearning for the outcome to have been different,
For some kind of reassurance.
It is the not knowing that is so troublesome.
There is a restlessness, a sense of something wrong always in the air,
That prevents sleep and concentration and living.

So the parent keeps vigil,
Praying and searching their heart and reliving,
Yelling out to God,
Trying to trust,
Hope against hope.

The dream is for the child to come home,
To be accepted and hugged and welcomed,
For all that was unsaid to be communicated,
And for forgiveness and love
To bring peace.

Meanwhile, the tears come again,
But God is in the midst
Even as we wait,
Encircling us with love and compassion,
And cradling us with grace.

Embarrassing ailments *(inspired by Luke 8:28)*

There are things we can barely tell ourselves
Never mind another human soul,
Things that bring shame and derision,
That cause us pain.

I had suffered for so many years,
Twelve years,
And I went to so many doctors,
And they were kind enough at the beginning
But their ideas didn't seem to work
And I was left alone again.

It is so frustrating, telling the same story so many times,
The questions, the tests, the scans,
And then at the end of it,
Still left with the same daily struggles.

People around me have stopped listening,
They don't seem to return my calls
Who wants to keep hearing the same
Complaint uttered over and over again.

If only I could find some-one to understand
Someone who would see me for who I am,
And who could bring healing.

I still have faith - it might just be the size of a grain of mustard
But I still hope, for relief, for peace.

Where can I find acceptance, and a welcoming presence
To find what I truly seek.

Jesus says: 'Daughter, your faith has healed you. Go in peace.'

In the storm I was so very fearful *(inspired by Luke 8:43-48)*

I thought I was ok – I had been through hard times before
I thought I had learned, had a new resilience.

But this time, it was just too much,
A time when my feet were pulled from under me,
And I was out in the wild landscape
The winds, the darkness, the turbulence
I felt disorientated and afraid,
What could it mean
What had I done to deserve this?
It was so unfair,
So bewildering.

The swell became more tumultuous,
The waves became bigger,
I was soaked and cold and the force of the water was so strong,
I felt that everything was falling apart,
I was so very fearful
With every wave,
I thought I would drown
All I could do was hold on.

And then a voice said, 'Why are you so afraid?'
And there was authority in his voice, 'Peace',
And all became calm.
The shadows and movement that had seemed so threatening
Lost their power,
And all became still.

'Be still and know that I am God.' (Psalm 46:10)

In the quietness, I found my courage once again
That I am never alone,
That I am being looked after by the King of the Universe,
And that whatever happens,
All is well.

Exhaustion – being strong for too long *(inspired by Mark 6:31)*

I am called to do this, it will be ok,
I can keep going, I will do my best
Many people have worse situations going on in their lives,
I can do this.

But as time goes by, it becomes more difficult
The giving up of seeing friends, of going out,
The sleepless nights, the worry,
The medical bills, the changes of carers,
It is getting harder.

My pride and stubbornness says that I can keep going,
It is a privilege to care,
That is what love is about,
Just a while longer.

There are awkward conversations,
People who don't understand
Rainy days of questioning and tears,
Of relentless fatigue and worry.

On the outside, the days look orderly and structured,
But on the inside, you are anxious,
What will happen if? You are risk managing
To make sure that all is well,
But the strain is so costly.

And then the invitation is made:
'Come with me by yourself, to a quiet place and get some rest.'

Could this be for real,
Relieved of the chains of responsibility and heightened alertness,
Just to be, to have space to breath,
To have a moment of rest,
Of being looked after, rather than looking after,
To experience a healing quiet and a deep peace.

May these times not be unusual,
For we need to built such spaces into our lives
For our wellbeing and sanity.

Time to rest, to be under that blanket, with that healing aroma
    and candle
With music or silent prayer or warm drink,
Time to rest, to catch our breath, to gather strength,
To enable us to come back into the responsibilities we must shoulder.

Being cradled by Jesus, and hearing his love song,
Brings restoration, repair and renewal, if only we come.

A FINAL WORD

I have a sense of privilege, for love songs have been playing all around us! Sometimes I have been making so much noise that I haven't even noticed. Sometimes I have tried to distract myself from the pain by immersing myself in other things. But then, I have caught a glimpse of heavenly harmonies, crescendos of melodies which have cascaded into my life, and filled me with an awareness that I am loved, and that there is a purpose in all this.

The angels have been singing with ethereal cadences, and every now and again I have been still enough to hear – as I have paused and noticed the beauty that is all around – even in the brokenness and unrelenting pain and trauma, even in illness and disability and despair.

I have been privileged to be surrounded with amazing people and places, and inspired songs and verse and writings. I have been heartened by the raw courage and loyalty and creativity of living in a community of people, whether I see them once a week or once every 20 years, people who have their own battles and heartbreaks, but who persevere, who find strength of God, so that somehow their hearts are still soft, still tender, after the most vile of experiences. As I have listened and prayed and wept, I have become more deeply aware of that transcendent and powerful love that encircles all of us, and offers us freedom to live once more, healing and hope. May the Holy Spirit give us ears to hear, and to rejoice and to live, and for our voice to join in the song.

> Don't let yourself forget that God's grace rewards not only those who never slip, but also those who bend and fall. So sing! The song of rejoicing softens hard hearts. It makes tears of godly sorrow flow from them. Singing summons the Holy Spirit. Happy praises offered in simplicity and love lead the faithful to complete harmony, without discord. Don't stop singing.
>
> Hildegard of Bingen (12th century)

PERMISSIONS

Thanks are expressed to the following Publishers for permission to use quotations from books mentioned:

Yale University Press with *Ever Yours* by Vincent van Gogh.

IVP with *Run with the Horses* by Eugene Peterson.

Pan Macmillan with *What Happened to You* by Oprah Winfrey.

Penguin Random House with *Braving the Wilderness* and *Rising Strong* by Brene Brown, and with *The Body Keeps the Score* by Bessel van der Kolk.

Darton, Longman and Todd with *The Wounded Healer* and *Here and Now Living in the Spirit* by Henri Nouwen.

We have sometimes found it impossible to trace copyright, and apologise to any Publishers who may have been inadvertently overlooked.

We are also grateful to Thank You Music who make their songs available free of copyright.

Bible quotations are normally from the NIV – *The Holy Bible, New International Version* © 1973, 1978, 1984, 2011 by Biblica inc. Used by permission. All rights reserved worldwide.

A few quotations are from *The Passion Translation*, © 2017, 2018, 2020 by Passion and Fire Ministries inc. TPT. Used by permission. All rights reserved.

Bible quotations marked NLT are taken from the *Holy Bible, New Living Translation*, © 1996, 2004, 2015 by Tyndale House Foundation. Used by permission of Tyndale House Publishers, Carol Stream, Illinois 60188. All rights reserved.

Bible quotations marked MSG are taken from *The Message*, © 1993, 2002, 2018 by Eugene H. Peterson. Used by permission of NavPress, represented by Tyndale House Pubishers. All rights reserved.